London's Parks & Countryside

Walks

*Originally compiled
by Brian Conduit
Revised by Deborah King*

Acknowledgements

Our thanks for the valuable advice and numerous useful leaflets obtained from Surrey County Council, the London Walking Forum, Hainault Forest Country Park, Bromley Council, Ewell Library and the various tourist information centres throughout the area.

Text:	Brian Conduit, Leigh Hatts, David Foster
	Revised text for 2010 edition, Deborah King
Photography:	Brian Conduit and Deborah King, pages 93 and
	95 Kevin Freeborn; front cover © iStockphoto.com/whitemay
Editor:	Ark Creative (UK) Ltd
Designer:	Ark Creative (UK) Ltd

This product includes mapping data licensed from Ordnance Survey® with the permission of the Controller of Her Majesty's Stationery Office. © Crown Copyright 2010. All rights reserved. Licence number 150002047. Ordnance Survey, the OS symbol and Pathfinder are registered trademarks and Explorer, Landranger and Outdoor Leisure are trademarks of the Ordnance Survey, the national mapping agency of Great Britain.

ISBN: 978-1-85458-513-4

While every care has been taken to ensure the accuracy of the route directions, the publishers cannot accept responsibility for errors or omissions, or for changes in details given. The countryside is not static: hedges and fences can be removed, field boundaries can alter, footpaths can be rerouted and changes in ownership can result in the closure or diversion of some concessionary paths. Also, paths that are easy and pleasant for walking in fine conditions may become slippery, muddy and difficult in wet weather, while stepping stones across rivers and streams may become impassable.

If you find an inaccuracy in either the text or maps, please write to Crimson Publishing at the address below.

First published 1999 as *In and Around London*; revised and reprinted 2003 and 2006.
Printed in Singapore. 5/10

First published in Great Britain 2010 by Crimson Publishing, a division of:
Crimson Business Ltd,
Westminster House, Kew Road, Richmond, Surrey, TW9 2ND

www.totalwalking.co.uk

A catalogue record for this book is available from the British library.

Front cover: Greenwich Park
Previous page: Hampton Court formal garden

Contents

 Up to 2 hours
Short walks on generally clear paths

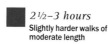 2½–3 hours
Slightly harder walks of moderate length

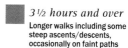 3½ hours and over
Longer walks including some steep ascents/descents, occasionally on faint paths

The walk times are provided as a guide only and are calculated using an average walking speed of 2½mph (4km/h), adding one minute for each 10m (33ft) of ascent, and then rounding the result to the nearest half hour.

Walks are considered to be dog friendly unless specified.

Keymap

SCALE 1:250 000 or 1 INCH to 4 MILES *1CM to 2.5KM*

KILOMETRES

MILES

KEYMAP HEIGHTS SHOWN IN METRES

At-a-glance

Walk	Page	Start	Nat. Grid Reference	Distance	Time	Height Gain
Ashtead Common	18	Ashtead Station	TQ 180590	3 miles (5km)	1½ hrs	150ft (45m)
Banstead Wood and Park Downs	40	Chipstead, Holly Lane	TQ 273583	4½ miles (7.2km)	2½ hrs	325ft (100m)
Belhus Woods Country Park	16	Belhus Woods Visitor Centre	TQ 565824	3 miles (4.8km)	1½ hrs	n/a
Bexley and Joyden's Wood	61	Bexley Station	TQ 493734	5½ miles (8.2km)	2½ hrs	235ft (70m)
Biggin Hill	73	Biggin Hill, Recreation Ground	TQ 419589	6½ miles (10.5km)	3 hrs	460ft (140m)
Blackheath and Greenwich Park	46	Blackheath Station	TQ 396760	5 miles (8km)	2½ hrs	165ft (50m)
Cassiobury Park and Whippendell Wood	67	Cassiobury Park	TQ 092967	6 miles (9.7km)	3 hrs	215ft (65m)
Chelsea and Battersea Park	26	Chelsea, Sloane Square	TQ 280786	4 miles (6.4km)	2 hrs	n/a
Colne Valley, South Hare-field and Bayhurst Wood	79	Denham Country Park	TQ 047864	7 miles (11.3km)	3½ hrs	360ft (110m)
Cudham and Downe	86	High Elms Country Park	TQ 446634	8 miles (12.9km)	4 hrs	755ft (230m)
Dagnam Park, Havering	12	Dagnam Park Nature Reserve	TQ 550927	2 miles (3.2km)	1 hr	n/a
Enfield Chase	28	Trent Country Park	TQ 281969	4 miles (6.4km)	2 hrs	260ft (80m)
Epping Forest	64	Queen Elizabeth's Hunting Lodge	TQ 397947	6 miles (9.7km)	3 hrs	360ft (110m)
Esher Common, Oxshott Heath & West End Common	76	West End Common, Esher	TQ 125626	7 miles (11.3km)	3½ hrs	280ft (85m)
Farthing Downs and Happy Valley	70	Farthing Downs, Coulsdon South	TQ 301571	6 miles (9.6km)	3 hrs	460ft (140m)
Hainault Forest	49	Hainault Forest Country Park	TQ 476926	5 miles (8km)	2½ hrs	280ft (85m)
Hampstead Heath	37	Hampstead Station	TQ 264858	4½ miles (7.2km)	2½ hrs	395ft (120m)
Hampton Court and Bushy parks	55	Hampton Court Station	TQ 153684	5½ miles (8.9km)	2½ hrs	n/a
Horsenden Hill	14	Horsenden Lane	TQ 160844	2½ miles (4km)	1½ hrs	195ft (60m)
Little Venice, Regent's Park and Primrose Hill	52	Little Venice	TQ 261818	5½ miles (8.9km)	2½ hrs	130ft (40m)
Marden Park Woods	43	Woldingham Station	TQ 359563	4½ miles (7.2km)	2½ hrs	410ft (125m)
Osterley Park and the Grand Union Canal	30	Osterley Park	TQ 147778	4½ miles (7.2km)	2 hrs	n/a
Richmond Park	82	Richmond Station	TQ 180751	8 miles (13km)	4 hrs	425ft (130m)
Royal parks and palaces of Central London	23	Parliament Square	TQ 300796	4 miles (6.5km)	2 hrs	n/a
Ruislip Woods and Lido	58	Ruislip Lido	TQ 087892	5½ miles (8.9km)	3 hrs	230ft (70m)
Totteridge and Mill Hill	34	The Ridgeway	TQ 224928	4½ miles (7.2km)	2 hrs	325ft (100m)
Wanstead Park	32	Wanstead Station	TQ 406882	4½ miles (7.2km)	2 hrs	n/a
Wimbledon Common	20	Wimbledon Common Windmill	TQ 230724	3½ miles (5.6km)	1½ hrs	160ft (50m)

Comments

A relaxing walk through the woodland and common with fine views and a pub well placed on the route.

There are many fine wooded stretches and a sense of remoteness on this walk on the North Downs.

Its flatness and number of seating areas along the route makes this walk ideal for all ages and abilities. It includes a conservation area teeming with birdlife and some lovely clumps of woodland.

This walk features a delightful stretch of the London Loop path adjacent to the River Cray and also passes through ancient Joyden's Wood.

The walk passes through several fine wooded areas, and there are extensive views across the North Downs to the Kent Weald.

The circuit of Greenwich Park, with its rich assortment of grand buildings, beautiful gardens and fine views over the Thames, is especially memorable.

A combination of parkland, woodland and waterway walking beside the River Gade and Grand Union Canal makes for a most satisfying and varied walk.

The varied architectural attractions of Chelsea on the north side of the Thames contrast with the more rural pleasures of Battersea Park on the south side of the river.

Pleasant canal walking and some delightful woodlands are combined with a visit to an attractive old church.

From a most attractive starting point, the route passes through some delightful woodland, two villages – with medieval churches – and the house in which Charles Darwin lived and worked.

A lovely walk through a nature reserve that comprises ancient woodland and parkland.

This is a pleasant figure-of-eight walk through the woodlands and across the grassland of Trent Country Park, one of the few remaining areas of Enfield Chase.

The dense woodlands and open grasslands of Epping Forest, an invaluable recreational amenity on the east side of London, are among the finest in the country.

This figure-of-eight walk explores three adjacent commons, which make up one of the largest remaining areas of heathland within the circumference of the M25.

This walk offers grand views across the downs, superb woodlands and an isolated and attractive medieval church.

Despite the proximity of north-east London, there are some grand views over the Essex countryside and some splendid areas of woodland.

The nearest real country walk to the centre of London, across rough heath and through woodland, that includes an 18th-century mansion and a fine viewpoint.

An invigorating walk across parkland and beside the Thames that has the magnificent Hampton Court Palace as its chief focal point.

Wooded slopes, a fine viewpoint, meadowland and a peaceful stretch of the Grand Union Canal make up a surprisingly rural walk in the heart of suburban west London.

A highly attractive stretch of the Regent's Canal is followed by a circuit of Regent's Park and a short and easy climb to the superb viewpoint of Primrose Hill.

A series of delightful woodlands and extensive views across the North Downs are the chief ingredients of this walk.

From the rural surroundings of Osterley Park and its great house, the route follows a stretch of the Grand Union Canal through the Brent River Park, passing one of Brunel's engineering triumphs.

An attractive stretch of the Thames Path is followed by the marvellous view from Henry VIII's Mound and a ramble across the heathland of Richmond Park.

A series of parks and palaces are linked on a green walk in the heart of London – a walk steeped in English tradition, pageantry and history.

The beautiful Ruislip Woods, remnants of the old forest of Middlesex, provide enjoyable walking in a largely suburban area.

This attractive walk follows a brook and includes an area of ancient hay meadows and the route is surprisingly rural.

Despite the proximity to the North Circular this is a charming walk through Wanstead Park, the grounds to a former manor house with royal connections.

The wide expanses of grassland and delightful wooded areas on Wimbledon Common provide pleasant and easy walking.

Introduction to London's Parks & Countryside

The walks in this guide are all contained within the circumference of the M25 motorway. They make up an unusually varied collection, and many people including Londoners, visitors and those wishing to stretch their legs during a long car journey, may well be surprised by how much open, attractive and unspoilt countryside still survives in an area that is often considered to comprise little more than sprawling suburbs and congested roads with little to offer walkers. You are about to discover some charming and delightful routes in the pages that follow.

The walks include some specially chosen routes in London and these use a combination of roads, riverside promenades and parks. Many have remarked that London's chief glory, and the thing that sets it apart from other European capitals, is its splendid expanses of parkland. Top of the list are the four adjacent royal parks of St James's, Green Park, Hyde Park and Kensington Gardens, which cut a huge green swathe across the very heart of the capital. Henry VIII originally enclosed most of them as deer parks, and they have been open to the public since at least the reign of Charles II. A little farther away is Regent's Park, also enclosed by Henry VIII but created in its present form by John Nash, with the support and encouragement of the Prince Regent. At Greenwich to the east is the oldest of the royal parks, while to the west are the adjacent parks of Hampton Court and Bushey and the largest of them all, Richmond, with its keyhole protected view across to St Paul's Cathedral.

In addition there are other parks and open spaces – large and small – ranging

Pond at West End village green

Horse Guards Parade

from the wild and hilly expanses of Hampstead Heath and the grassland and woodland of Wimbledon Common, to the traditional ornamental gardens of Battersea Park and the lovely grounds of the Royal Hospital Chelsea. Some of the walks make use of the Thames Path, a National Trail that follows England's best-known river from source to mouth. It enables people to enjoy attractive walks, from Richmond in the west to Greenwich in the east, mainly along traffic-free riverside paths and embankments on both sides of the river. The Thames has always been a major artery, and the easiest form of transport in the past, which is why so many royal and other palaces were built near its banks. Some walks take you through oases or narrow fingers of greenery in predominantly suburban areas – Horsenden Hill, Ruislip Woods and the Brent River Park are three such examples – that either managed to survive, or have been reclaimed from, the rapid expansion of housing, roads and industry that took place especially in the 1930s. The remainder of the walks are in the rural fringes just beyond the boundaries of the capital – Epping Forest and Enfield Chase, the Surrey heathlands and North Downs. Many of these have an unexpected solitude and tranquility normally experienced only in the more thinly populated and remote parts of Britain and give the impression that both the M25 and London's suburbs are hundreds of miles away.

The suburbs of London
At first glance suburban London might not sound promising territory for walking as it lacks the rural appeal of the green belt but there are many lovely walks to be found here. The riverside meadows by some of London's lesser-known rivers such as the Colne, Lee, Pinn, Brent and Dollis Brook, provide pleasant walking, and some sizeable remnants of the forests that once surrounded London still survive amid the housing, preserving something of the pastoral landscape of 'Rural Middlesex', whose destruction was so much

lamented by the poet John Betjeman.

Several walks make use of the Grand Union Canal, which starts its journey to Birmingham in the heart of London behind Paddington Station. From here it winds its way through the western and north-western parts of London, before continuing into the more open Hertfordshire countryside. One attractive feature that walkers in London will soon realise is the extent to which some of the small towns and villages that have been engulfed by the city's growth retain something of their formal rural atmosphere, with large greens where cricket is still often played, traditional pubs, picturesque cottages and old churches. Hampstead, Blackheath, Wimbledon and parts of Chelsea immediately spring to mind, and farther westwards along the Thames, Richmond still reminds us that it was once a quiet riverside settlement.

Rich in wildlife

Some of the walks are in areas and along paths that provide particularly good habitats for plants and wildlife. The Dollis Valley Greenwalk, near Mill Hill, is one such example, where you might spot a kingfisher and the nearby ancient grassland of Totteridge Fields attracts hoards of butterflies. Kingfishers can also be seen along the River Cray, near to Bexley, and Belhus Woods Country Park offers a valuable habitat for invertebrates, as well as conservation areas for birds. The Anglo Saxons once inhabited some of our ancient woodlands and some of the earthworks they constructed are still noticeable, including Faesten Dic, in Joyden's Wood, which was built to defend them against their enemies in London. Another is Loughton Camp, an earthwork found in Epping Forest. Ashtead Common is home to an array of wildlife such as owls, woodpeckers and butterflies and its ancient woodland is also the site of a 2nd century AD Roman villa and bathhouse.

Local councils and local campaign groups have helped to safeguard many areas that would otherwise have become overgrown and neglected. Dagnam Park near to Harold Wood is a perfect example of how ancient woodland and its environs has been transformed into a nature reserve. Wanstead Park's ornamental lakes and surrounding grassland were once the grounds to a house so grand it was considered in its day to rival Hampton Court Palace. The house was owned by one of the richest women in England but although her husband squandered her fortune, the grounds survive and form one of the walks in this book. The M25 may be close to some of the walks but they are surprisingly tranquil and give a real sense of walking in the footsteps of our predecessors.

Farther afield

Beyond the suburbs but still within the M25 there is a relatively narrow rural area, within which a surprising amount of open countryside remains. In the Middle Ages, London was surrounded on all sides by huge areas of thick forest and rough heath, and there are still quite substantial remains of these. Of the once vast forest of Essex, Epping and Hainault provide excellent walking facilities, and fragments of the old Forest of Middlesex survive at Enfield Chase and Ruislip Woods.

Some of the finest and most unspoilt country near the capital is to be found on the North Downs in Surrey and Kent. From the well-wooded downland slopes, the views often extend from the Thames Basin to the lush and sylvan pastures of the Weald. In western Surrey, areas of the rough and inhospitable heathland, once so detested and feared by travellers, still survive amid the affluence and large houses of Esher and Oxshott.

Osterley Park – a great house and estate in Greater London

For the preservation of at least some of these rural landscapes – both as segments of unspoilt countryside and as places for public recreation and enjoyment – we have to thank the Corporation of the City of London, who have protected them from development since Victorian times. Two such areas are Epping Forest north of Chingford and Farthing Downs just to the south of Croydon. Two regional parks based on rivers – the Colne in west London and the Lee in east London – have been established to preserve and enhance the rural landscape of those valleys and provide a range of recreational amenities.

Walking in the area

Apart from the Thames Path, there are a number of other well-waymarked routes in and around London. Many of the walks use stretches of the London Loop, a 150-mile (241km) route that passes through some of the finest rural areas of the Home Counties. 'Loop' stands for London Outer Orbital Path, which is the walker's equivalent of the M25. Both this and the inner orbital route – the Capital Ring – total 221 miles (356km) in length and are connected to the London Walks Network, which was developed by the London Walking Forum. These initiatives will only add to the already extensive network of attractive and well-waymarked routes already available to walkers both within and around Britain's capital city.

This book includes a list of waypoints alongside the description of the walk, so that you can enjoy the full benefits of gps should you wish to. For more information on using your gps, read the *Pathfinder® Guide GPS for Walkers,* by gps teacher and navigation trainer, Clive Thomas (ISBN 978-0-7117-4445-5). For essential information on map reading and basic navigation, read the *Pathfinder® Guide Map Reading Skills* by outdoor writer, Terry Marsh (ISBN 978-0-7117-4978-8). Both titles are available in bookshops or can be ordered online at www.totalwalking.co.uk

Dagnam Park, Havering

Start	Dagnam Park Nature Reserve car park at the end of Settle Road
Distance	2 miles (3.2km) [add ½ mile if joining the walk from the bus stop in Settle Road]
Height gain	Negligible
Approximate time	1 hour
Public transport	Train to Harold Wood, then bus no. 294 and alight at Settle Road bus stop
Route terrain	Parkland with some woodland paths
Ordnance Survey maps	Landranger 177 (East London), Explorer 175 (Southend-on-Sea & Basildon)

GPS waypoints

- TQ 550 927
- Ⓐ TQ 549 926
- Ⓑ TQ 546 931
- Ⓒ TQ 544 935
- Ⓓ TQ 551 929

This walk takes you through Dagnam Park, a site of around 184 acres and once home to three manor houses. One of these had a 16th century Elizabethan moat and part of this can still be seen today. Thanks to campaigning from the local group Friends of Dagnam Park, much of the park is now a nature reserve and despite its proximity to the M25 the area is surprisingly peaceful. You will pass through ancient woodland and wildflower meadows and you're quite likely to see deer in neighbouring fields.

Begin at the Dagnam Park Nature Reserve sign at the approach to the car park and at the fork bear left along a

Deer beside footpath in Dagnam Park

path. After 20 yds, at a gap in the wooden fencing, turn left along a wide grassy path and head for the trees. Turn left along a path, with a pond on your right, and continue towards the backs

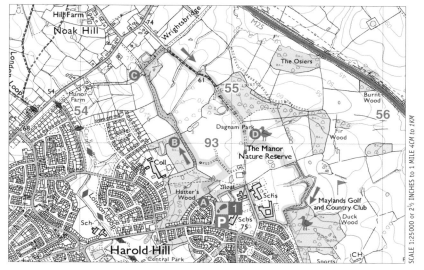

SCALE 1:25 000 or 2½ INCHES to 1 MILE 4CM to 1KM

of some houses. To your left is the moat that surrounded the Elizabethan house. This is now a scheduled ancient monument and a breeding ground for great crested newts. Just before you reach the garden wall of a house turn right **A**, and pass to the left of a pond. Continue to skirt the pond and just before the car park on your right, turn left to join a tarmac path on the edge of parkland.

Where the path ends in front of a circle of trees, bear left towards woodland and then turn right along a grassy path beside the woodland. Go through a hedge gap beside a metal gate. At a crossing of paths turn left **B** along a stony path and head into the thin belt of woodland. Turn right and continue ahead looking out for deer in the grassland on either side. Just past some wooden fencing look out for a public footpath signpost and turn right in the direction of Lower Noak Close **C**.

Keep ahead along the enclosed path, passing a pond, to reach a tarmac lane. Turn right here and pass beside a metal gate to join a sandy track used by both walkers and cyclists. This section of the walk is the only time that traffic from

the M25 is apparent. You will later pass the white gateposts to a Georgian mansion dating from 1772. Before its demise in the 1950s it was home to Sir Richard Neave, governor of the Bank of England, who employed the leading Victorian garden designer, Humphrey Repton, as well as 40 servants.

Keep ahead until you reach the end of the hedgerow scrub, about 200 yds before the sandy track ends, where you turn left **D**, uphill along a grassy path. Pass to the left of a pond, head downhill to enter a spinney and keep along the main path to the right of a golf course. Cross a brook, bear right along a meandering uphill path, and continue along the embankment as the path descends into Duck Wood, an ancient woodland and an important site for nature conservation.

Cross a brook and bear right to pass beside a wooden gate to exit the nature reserve. At the road turn right and at the T-junction with Settle Road, turn left to the bus stop or right to return to the car park. ●

Horsenden Hill

		GPS waypoints
Start	Horsenden Hill car park, at top of Horsenden Lane	⬛ TQ 160 844
Distance	2½ miles (4km). Add ¾ mile (1.2km) if coming from Perivale Station and pick up the walk at point Ⓓ	Ⓐ TQ 158 847 Ⓑ TQ 162 848 Ⓒ TQ 162 843 Ⓓ TQ 162 839 Ⓔ TQ 153 842
Height gain	195 feet (60m)	
Approximate time	1½ hours (2 hours from Perivale Station)	
Public transport	Underground to Perivale (Central line). Turn right to pass under the railway bridge, keep ahead and, on approaching a canal bridge, turn right down steps to the towpath to join the main walk at point Ⓓ	
Route terrain	Open grassland, canal paths	
Ordnance Survey maps	Landranger 176 (West London), Explorer 173 (London North)	

Horsenden Hill rises to 279 feet above West London, with extensive fine views from the summit. Together with the adjoining meadows, which run down to the Grand Union Canal, this unspoilt rural oasis has managed to survive amid a predominantly suburban landscape. Much of this route follows the Capital Ring recreational path through an attractive combination of woodland and meadowland, with a pleasant stretch along the canal towpath.

The Grand Union Canal below Horsenden Hill

For the almost miraculous preservation of this small but intensely valuable area of countryside, we are indebted to Middlesex County Council, who bought it as a public recreation area when surrounding suburban expansion was at its height in the 1930s. Now it is maintained by Ealing Borough Council.

🔖 Start by walking back towards the road but, just before it, turn right on to a tarmac path that heads downhill, keeping parallel to the road (Horsenden Lane) and emerging on to it by the **Ballot Box pub**. Keep ahead in front of the pub and just beyond it turn right onto the Capital Ring along a tree-lined tarmac path **Ⓐ**. Follow it as far as a metal barrier, where you turn right to enter Horsenden Wood **Ⓑ**.

Immediately take the left-hand path at a fork, cross a track and keep ahead, climbing gently all the while. Turn right on joining another path, continue uphill along the right edge of a golf course and, when you see the triangulation pillar that marks the summit, turn left to head across to it **Ⓒ**. The contrasting views from here are superb: looking eastwards across the mass of built-up London and westwards over the suburbs towards the more rural delights of the distant Chilterns.

Continue past the triangulation pillar, making for the right corner of the open grassy area on the top of Horsenden Hill, and take a path that leads down steps and winds through thick wood-land to emerge from the trees. Go over a stile and keep along the right edge of rough grassland to reach a crossing of grassy paths, just after passing to the right of a solitary oak tree. Turn left downhill into trees again, go through a kissing-gate and ascend steps to a road and turn left to cross a footbridge over the Grand Union Canal. *If returning to Perivale Station, continue along the road.*

Just after crossing the canal bridge, turn left **Ⓓ** down steps to the towpath and turn left along it, passing under the bridge. Keep along the towpath, with Perivale Wood on your left, and pass under a wooden footbridge. Here

the route leaves the Capital Ring; turn left **Ⓔ** through a metal gate, at a public footpath sign, along a path that curves left uphill to a T-junction. Turn sharp left to cross the bridge – ahead is a fine view of Horsenden Hill – then turn first sharp right and then left to pass beside a metal barrier. Turn left on to a path that keeps along the right edge of a playing field, by a hedge and trees on the right, and in the field corner turn right through a gap in the line of trees.

Continue along the left edge of a meadow, pass through another gap, turn left by a hedge on the left and, in the corner of the meadow, bear left through trees to join a clear path. Head gently uphill along this tree-lined path, passing a blue-painted fingerpost. Turn left at a fork, go up steps on to a road, continue up the steps on the opposite side and turn right on to a tarmac path to return to the start.   ●

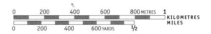

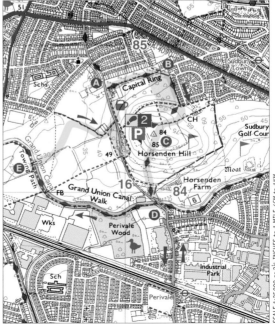

Belhus Woods Country Park

	GPS waypoints
Start Belhus Woods Visitor Centre car park (Pay and Display)	🖉 TQ 565 824
Distance 3 miles (4.8km)	Ⓐ TQ 564 825
	Ⓑ TQ 561 830
Height gain Negligible	Ⓒ TQ 569 827
Approximate time 1½ hours	Ⓓ TQ 573 823
Public transport Bus no. 373 from Grays to Romford passes the park, every half an hour	
Route terrain Country parkland and lakeside paths	
Dog friendly On a lead near lakes during the nesting season	
Ordnance Survey maps Landranger 177 (East London), Explorer 162 (Greenwich & Gravesend)	

This little walk is just three miles north of the Lakeside Shopping Centre and is well worth the detour. There are some delightful stretches of woodland and former gravel pits have been successfully transformed into a lakeland conservation area which is now a valuable wildlife habitat. You will also walk in the footsteps of prehistoric farmers as traces of Iron Age pottery and tool-making areas have been discovered between Ⓑ and Ⓒ. The grand Belhus mansion has long gone but its grounds are now an attractive country park with managed woodlands. Several of the areas are coppiced and the new growths of hazel form stems that are harvested every few years and used for making hedging stakes and walking sticks.

🖉 Begin at the car park beside the visitor centre and take the track opposite that leads to another parking area with a barbeque on the right. Turn left here towards the road on to a wide track and at the pedestrian crossing, cross the road (Romford Road) Ⓐ.

Immediately bear right along the field edge path and enter White Post Wood. After a few paces at a T-junction, bear right and follow this path as it meanders through woodland. At a fork bear left and at the next T-junction, bear right to a further T-junction beside a pylon. Turn left Ⓑ, and at the gravel path bear

left to return to the pedestrian crossing. Cross the road and turn left and the track veers away from the road and passes a lake with three islands which was successfully transformed from disused gravel pits into a conservation area. It is teeming with wildlife during early summer. At the T-junction turn right and after 100 yds, after a small pond, turn left to cross a wooden footbridge on the right Ⓒ. You have just crossed Running Water Brook, which is noted for its colony of water voles.

Take the left-hand fork along a grassy path to reach another conservation area

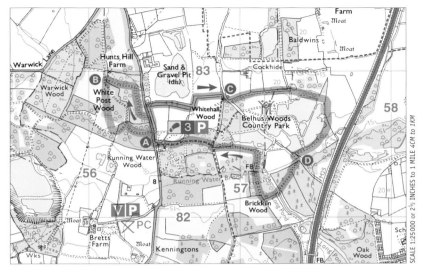

and keep the lake on your right as the path narrows. Continue around the lakes and go through a hedge gap and over a stile **D**.

Bear right along a delightful grassy path through a young plantation of native trees. Look out for dragonflies and butterflies in this area. After 200 yds you will pass to the right of Long Pond, once the focal point of the estate's landscape, designed by Capability Brown. Two centuries later the construction of the M25 divided the lake into two but it has now been restored to

Seat by conservation area, Belhus Woods

something like its former glory.

Pass beside a gate and keep ahead for 40 yds looking out for a squeezer-stile on the right. Go through and follow the path through Brickkiln Wood to eventually reach an open area beside the lakes. As the name suggests bricks were made from London Clay that was deposited beneath the sea 40 million years ago. There is evidence that bricks were first made here in the 17th century. Turn left along the gravel path back to the car park. ●

Ashtead Common

		GPS waypoints
Start	Ashtead Station car park (Pay and Display)	☑ TQ 180 590
Distance	3 miles (5km)	Ⓐ TQ 179 593
Height gain	150 feet (45m)	Ⓑ TQ 178 606
Approximate time	1½ hours	Ⓒ TQ 167 598
Public transport	London Waterloo to Ashtead	
Route terrain	Woodland and grassland paths	
Dog friendly	Keep dogs on a lead near Wood Field during early summer (skylarks' nesting season)	
Ordnance Survey maps	Landranger 187 (Dorking & Reigate), Explorer 161 (London South)	

Ashtead Common is a mosaic of woodland, scrub and grassland and its ancient trees are renowned. The walk takes you through the ancient woodland, which is home to a host of wildlife including woodpeckers, owls and the Purple Emperor butterfly.

📝 From the station car park turn left, go over the level crossing and take the path ahead into Ashtead Common.

The common is highly regarded for its large collection of ancient trees, including around 2,300 oaks, and its invertebrates as more than 1,000 species of beetle have been recorded

Ashtead Common

here. Wood Field to your left is a popular nesting ground for skylarks during early summer. Cross a bridge over a stream and at the path junction bear right 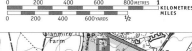 **A** to pass beside a blue waymarked post (bridleway 33).

Keep ahead all the time along a wide, grassy path, past two sets of crossways. Pass to the right of Flag Pond at the edge of the forest. West of this pond but not easy to spot are the remains of a Roman villa and bathhouse dating from the 1st and 2nd centuries AD. Excavations in the 1920s revealed a rare type of corridor villa that had two rows of six rooms behind the corridor, instead of the more usual single row, and evidence suggests there was a thriving tile industry here too.

At a public footpath sign, turn left in the direction of Kingston Road **B**.

Notice the white London boundary marker post on the right here. Keep ahead as the path ascends while over to the right there are extensive views of arable land. You are now following bridleway 29 and after a mile the path descends to a fork by an Ashtead Common information board.

To visit **The Star pub** turn right here, along Epsom Gap, and cross the road. The pub is then on your right.

However, to continue the walk turn left **C** and follow the path (concessionary Ride 1) to the bridge at point **A** from where you can retrace your steps to the start of the walk. ●

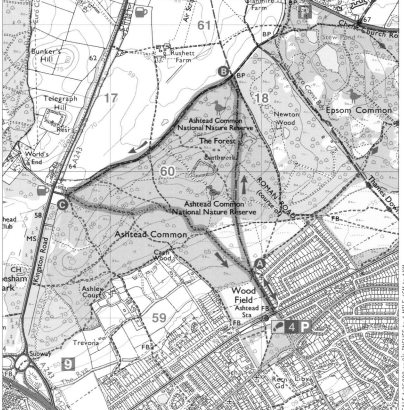

Wimbledon Common

		GPS waypoints
Start	Wimbledon Common Windmill, at end of Windmill Road	TQ 230 724
Distance	3½ miles (5.6km). Add 1½ miles (2.4km) if coming from Wimbledon Station and pick up the walk at point Ⓑ	Ⓐ TQ 230 722 Ⓑ TQ 235 712 Ⓒ TQ 228 716 Ⓓ TQ 222 711 Ⓔ TQ 225 726
Height gain	160 feet (50m)	
Approximate time	1½ hours (2½ hours from Wimbledon Station)	
Parking	Car park by Wimbledon Common Windmill	
Public transport	Trains from London (Waterloo) or Underground to Wimbledon (District line). Turn right, head up Wimbledon Hill Road to a T-junction and turn right along High Street through Wimbledon village. Turn left at the next T-junction, continue along Parkside to the common and at a fork by a war memorial take the left-hand road. After crossing a road you join the main walk	
Route terrain	Parkland and woodland	
Ordnance Survey maps	Landranger 176 (West London), Explorer 161 (London South)	

First-time visitors who expect smooth expanses of grassy parkland are in for something of a shock for much of Wimbledon Common, and the adjacent Putney Heath to the north, comprise rough heathland and thick woodland – a genuinely rural oasis amid suburban south London. The walk does a circuit of the common and passes by the remains of a prehistoric fort and several ponds. There are plenty of refreshment facilities in nearby Wimbledon village, easily reached from point Ⓑ.

In the past Wimbledon Common seems to have been a favourite venue for duelling; the last one occurred in 1840. It extends over 1,000 acres and has been protected by an Act of Parliament since 1871. Wimbledon Common Windmill was erected in 1817 on the site of an earlier one. A plaque states that Lord Baden-Powell wrote part of his *Scouting for Boys* while living here.

From the Windmill, walk back along the road to a junction, turn right and pass beside a metal barrier. Keep ahead along a straight track, take the first path on the left Ⓐ and follow it across the common, initially along the right edge of open grassland and later between trees, to a road.

Walkers returning to Wimbledon Station should cross over and continue along the track ahead to the war memorial, where they pick up the outward route

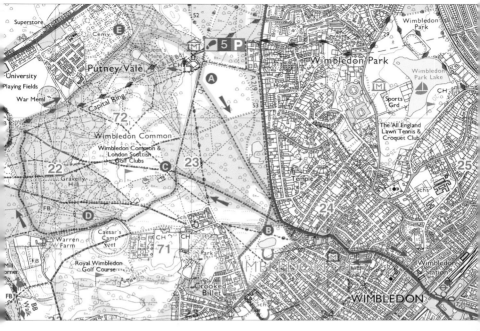

and retrace their steps to the station.

Turn right on to a path alongside the road and, where a riding track crosses the road about 100 yds before reaching the Causeway, turn sharp right **B** on to a path that keeps parallel to this riding track on the right. Cross a road and keep ahead through trees and across rough

Queen's Mere

grassland – ignoring all side turns – until the path emerges into a more open area at a major crossing of paths and tracks **C**. Turn left along a broad track, which curves right across part of the Royal Wimbledon Golf Course, to a fork and continue along the left-hand track

Wimbledon Common Windmill

to reach a tarmac drive.

Cross over, walk along the track opposite towards trees and, on entering them, follow the track downhill beside a wire fence by the golf course. The path curves left to continue through this delightful woodland. The tree-covered low mound on the left is all that remains of Caesar's Camp which, despite its name, is a prehistoric fort. It was badly damaged by a Victorian owner of the site.

Look out for a fork, where you take the right-hand track **D** – passing between three upright concrete posts – which heads gently downhill, initially keeping parallel to the other track but then curving right. Keep on the main track all the while, which later curves right again to continue along the left, inside edge of the common. The buildings of Putney Vale can be seen to the left, and later the track keeps along the right edge of a cemetery.

Where a path leads off to the right over a brick culvert in a ditch **E** – it leaves the track opposite a gate into the cemetery – follow it to the attractive and secluded Queen's Mere. On the left side of the pool, turn left, at a blue post waymarked with a fish and arrow, on to an uphill path through woodland. Bear right, following the regular waymarked posts, and the path emerges on to open grassland by the windmill. ●

Royal parks and palaces of Central London

		GPS waypoints
Start	Parliament Square	🖉 TQ 300 796
Finish	Kensington High Street	Ⓐ TQ 295 797
Distance	4 miles (6.5km)	Ⓑ TQ 294 801
Height gain	Negligible	Ⓒ TQ 289 802
Approximate time	2 hours	Ⓓ TQ 284 298
Public transport	Underground to Westminster (District, Circle and Northern lines), return from High Street Kensington (Circle and District lines)	Ⓔ TQ 268 801
		Ⓕ TQ 266 806
		Ⓖ TQ 259 800
Route terrain	Parkland	
Ordnance Survey maps	Landranger 176 (West London), Explorer 173 (London North)	

The adjacent royal parks of St James's, the Green, Hyde and Kensington Gardens make up a huge green block in the very heart of the capital. This route links the four parks and the various royal palaces associated with them, enabling you to enjoy an almost entirely rural walk from the Palace of Westminster, better known as the Houses of Parliament, to Kensington Palace across continuous parkland and for the most part away from traffic. On the way you catch a glimpse of Buckingham Palace and pass by St James's Palace.

Parliament Square contains statues of several great national leaders, including one of Churchill in a typically belligerent wartime pose. He is facing the vast bulk of the Houses of Parliament, built in the middle of the 19th century to the designs of Sir Charles Barry and Augustus Pugin after most of its predecessor was destroyed by fire in 1834. The buildings stand on the site of the medieval royal palace of Westminster but little of this survived the fire apart from the late 11th-century Westminster Hall. The hall has been the setting for a number of famous trials,

including those of Guy Fawkes in 1605 and Charles I in 1649. It is particularly noted for its magnificent 14th-century hammerbeam roof.

On the other side of the road stands Westminster Abbey. Since the original Saxon minster was rebuilt by Edward the Confessor shortly before the Norman Conquest, it has been the coronation place of English monarchs, and many are also buried here. The present church dates mainly from the 13th century, when it was extensively rebuilt again by Henry III. The Henry VII Chapel at the east end was added in the early 16th century, and the abbey was heavily restored by Wren and Hawksmoor in the early 18th century. Apart from the royal tombs, the interior contains a huge number of memorials to statesmen, writers, artists, soldiers, scientists and others, including the tomb of the Unknown Warrior. Plenty of time needs to be devoted to a visit to this vast repository of much of the nation's history.

Start from the north side of Parliament Square and walk along Parliament Street towards the Cenotaph. Turn left into King Charles Street, walking between the imposing government buildings of the Treasury to the left and the Foreign and Commonwealth Office to the right, and descend steps by the statue of Robert Clive (Clive of India). To the left is the entrance to the underground Cabinet War Rooms. This is where meetings of the Wartime Cabinet were held and where Churchill used to sleep throughout the Blitz.

Cross the road into St James's Park and turn right on to a path that curves left to keep beside the lake. To the right is a fine view across Horse Guards Parade. Walk beside the lake as far as a crossing of paths to the right of a bridge **Ⓐ**. The views from the bridge – looking towards Whitehall in one direction and the façade of Buckingham Palace in the other – are most impressive. Turn right at the crossroads to emerge on to the Mall, cross over and take the road opposite, passing between St James's Palace on the left and the Queen's Chapel on the right. The latter was completed in the early 17th century by Inigo Jones for Queen Henrietta Maria, wife of Charles I.

Turn left along Pall Mall **Ⓑ** to pass in front of St James's Palace. This mainly Tudor structure, built by Henry VIII, was the principal royal residence until superseded by Buckingham Palace in the reign of George IV; foreign ambassadors are still accredited to the Court of St James's. At the end of Pall Mall, keep ahead along Cleveland Row – Clarence House is to the left – pass to the right of Selwyn House and keep ahead along a path into the Green Park. Turn left to pass by the early 19th-century Lancaster House, take the first turning on the right and, at a junction of three paths, turn sharply right to continue across the park. Bear right on joining another path and, before reaching Piccadilly, turn left **Ⓒ** to continue along the right edge of the park to Hyde Park Corner.

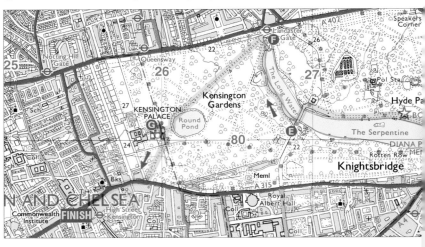

Here turn right 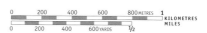 to cross the road to the island via the pedestrian crossing and bear right, passing to the right of a statue of the Duke of Wellington. The 'Iron Duke' is appropriately overlooking Apsley House, a fine Georgian mansion that was his London residence. Then go under the Hyde Park Corner Subway, following signs to Hyde Park, and on emerging from it, turn left and left again to pass through the gates into the park.

Cross a road, turn left along a path that runs parallel to the sandy riding-track of Rotten Row on the left and turn half-right to enter the Rose Garden. Continue through it, keep ahead to a T-junction, turn right to a more complex junction and turn left to follow a drive along the right edge of the Serpentine. Turn left to cross a bridge over it and turn right into Kensington Gardens .

At a junction, take the path to the right, signposted Peter Pan and Italian Fountain, which keeps close to the left bank of Long Water. Pass the well-known Peter Pan statue and continue to the delightful Italian Gardens on the right. Just before reaching the edge of the park, turn sharply left on to a path that cuts across the park to an obelisk, erected in 1864 to Speke, the explorer. Continue past it, following signs to Kensington Palace, to the Round Pond, follow the edge of the pond as it curves left and take the first turning on the right to the Broad Walk . In front is Kensington Palace and the statue of Queen Victoria, who was born in the palace in 1819 and first heard of her accession to the throne here 18 years later.

In 1689 William III and Mary II bought the modest Nottingham House that stood here and gave Wren the job of redesigning and enlarging it into the present Kensington Palace. For many years it was a principal royal residence and still has private apartments for members of the royal family. It was the home of Diana, Princess of Wales, and in the autumn of 1997 became the main focal point for the outpouring of public grief that followed her death.

Turn right if visiting the State Apartments and Orangery but the route continues to the left along the Broad Walk, laid out by Caroline of Anspach, wife of George II. Take the first path on the right, then turn left and walk diagonally across the park to emerge on to Kensington High Street. To the right is an imposing view of the main front of the palace and the statue of William III. Turn right along Kensington High Street to the Underground station. ●

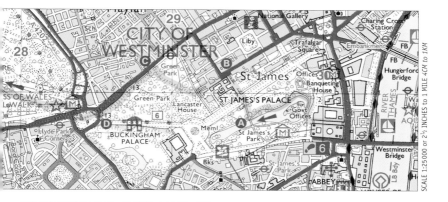

Chelsea and Battersea Park

		GPS waypoints	
Start	Chelsea, Sloane Square		
Distance	4 miles (6.4km)		TQ 280 786
Height gain	Negligible	Ⓐ	TQ 277 784
Approximate time	2 hours	Ⓑ	TQ 282 781
Public transport	Underground to Sloane Square (Circle and District lines)	Ⓒ	TQ 282 778
		Ⓓ	TQ 270 775
		Ⓔ	TQ 274 773
Route terrain	Pavements and parkland	Ⓕ	TQ 283 774
Ordnance Survey maps	Landranger 176 (West London), Explorer 161 (London South)	Ⓖ	TQ 285 776

From busy Sloane Square, a walk through the grounds and parkland surrounding the Royal Hospital at Chelsea leads down to the Thames and the Chelsea Embankment. Then follows an exploration of the delightful area around Cheyne Walk, before crossing Albert Bridge for a tour of part of Battersea Park on the south side of the river. You recross the Thames via Chelsea Bridge to return to the start. Note: The Royal Hospital Chelsea grounds are closed between April – June for the Chelsea Flower Show.

Start by walking through Sloane Square and on along King's Road. Turn left into Cheltenham Terrace Ⓐ, passing the early 19th-century Duke of York's Headquarters on the left, continue along Franklin's Row and at a T-junction by the Royal Hospital, keep ahead through London Gate into the hospital grounds. If these are closed, instead turn right and then left into Tite Street and at the Embankment rejoin directions from Ⓒ.

The Royal Hospital at Chelsea, designed by Wren, was founded in 1682 by Charles II as a retirement home for old and disabled soldiers. Today it houses over 400 'Chelsea Pensioners', resplendent in their distinctive scarlet coats and three-cornered hats. Pass beside Garden Gate, keep ahead along a broad, tree-lined drive and take the first path on the right Ⓑ to continue in front

of the south – the most impressive – façade of the hospital. In front of the gates, turn left along a gravel path and go through gates on to the Chelsea Embankment Ⓒ. Turn right beside the river towards Albert Bridge and, at traffic lights, turn right along Royal Hospital Road and then immediately left to continue along Cheyne Walk, lined with trees and dignified 18th-century houses.

Briefly rejoin the Embankment by Albert Bridge but then keep ahead along another section of Cheyne Walk. At the **Cheyne Walk Brasserie**, turn right along Cheyne Row, another delightful street of handsome and elegant houses. This area of Chelsea has always attracted writers and artists, and among those who have lived here are James McNeil Whistler, J.M. Turner, Bram Stoker, Hilaire Belloc, George Eliot, Thomas Carlyle and more

SCALE 1:25000 or 2½ INCHES to 1 MILE 4CM to 1KM

recently Mick Jagger. Carlyle's house – No. 24 – is now owned by the National Trust.

Turn left into Upper Cheyne Row, left again into Lawrence Street, turn right along Justice Walk and turn left along Old Church Street to Chelsea Old Church **D**. This ancient church, founded in the 12th century, was badly damaged in an air raid in 1941 and had to be almost rebuilt. It is particularly associated with Sir Thomas More who worshipped here; his statue is outside.

Continue to the left along the Embankment again to Albert Bridge and turn right over it. At a Riverside Walk sign, turn left through a gate into Battersea Park **E**. Walk initially beside the Thames and take the first tarmac path on the right. Turn left at a T-junction a few yards ahead and, about 50 yds after joining a broad drive, turn right down steps, and ahead is an attractive view over the park, created in 1853 from former marshland. Make for a small rectangular pool, pass along its right side, go up steps and keep ahead,

bearing slightly right, to a T-junction.

Turn left to the next junction of paths and turn left again along a broad, tree-lined drive, passing a bandstand and continuing to the edge of a boating lake. To the right is a 19th-century pump house, now a gallery and information centre for the park. Walk alongside the lake, go through a gate on to a broad drive, turn left and take the first path on the right **F**. The path, passing between tennis courts on the left and a running track on the right, bears gradually right to a drive.

Turn right along the drive and turn left **G** to recross the Thames by Chelsea Bridge. Look back here for a view of Battersea Power Station, built in 1934 and now redundant. Keep ahead along Chelsea Bridge Road – on the left are the grounds of the Royal Hospital and on the right are army barracks – and continue along Lower Sloane Street to return to Sloane Square. ●

Enfield Chase

		GPS waypoints
Start	Trent Country Park car park	🖉 TQ 281 969
Distance	4 miles (6.4km). Add ¾ mile (1.2km) if coming from Cockfosters Station	Ⓐ TQ 286 966 Ⓑ TQ 288 970 Ⓒ TQ 288 975
Height gain	260 feet (80m)	Ⓓ TQ 293 975
Approximate time	2 hours (2½ hours from Cockfosters)	Ⓔ TQ 286 981 Ⓕ TQ 281 976
Public transport	Underground to Cockfosters (Piccadilly line). Turn right along the main road, turn right through the entrance to Trent Country Park and follow the drive to the car park	
Route terrain	Grassy paths, woodland	
Ordnance Survey maps	Landranger 166 (Luton & Hertford), Explorer 173 (London North)	

Trent Country Park is a remnant of the ancient royal hunting ground of Enfield Chase, which once extended over nearly 8,000 acres of north Middlesex, part of the extensive woodlands that surrounded much of the capital. This easy paced walk is a pleasant mixture of woodland and grassland and includes a lake, water gardens and a glimpse of Trent House, now part of Middlesex University.

🖉 The walk starts in the car park, at the information board by the **café**. Walk back along the drive, go through the gates of the car park and, just beyond a monument (which informs you that the gardens were begun in 1706) and a 'Welcome to Trent Country Park' board, turn left, at a London Loop waymarked post. Head across the grass to the next post and continue along the left edge of a field, by woodland on the left. Bear left into the wood – Church Wood – follow a winding path through it, turn right at a waymarked post and bear left to emerge from the trees.

Keep ahead across a field, cross a footbridge over a ditch and, at the next London Loop post, turn left – here leaving the 'Loop' – and walk along the left edge of a field. Continue through a line of trees and on across the next field, heading gently downhill. In the field corner, turn left Ⓐ on to a path that gently ascends along the right, inside edge of Church Wood and turn right at a T-junction along a straight, tree-lined path.

Pass beside a gate, turn left at the junction Ⓑ and turn left again at the next junction. Just past an obelisk turn right beside a barrier, go through a kissing-gate and follow a track through woodland. The track later emerges into open country. Turn right and keep parallel to the edge of a lake and at a fork Ⓒ take the right-hand track – for a short detour to the Water Garden – and Trent House can be seen to the right

In Trent Country Park

above the lake.

The house has certainly had a variety of roles. Originally a small 18th-century villa, it was rebuilt on a more grandiose scale by the Sassoon family in the early 20th century. During the Second World War it was used as an interrogation centre for high-ranking German prisoners and now it is part of Middlesex University.

The path curves right alongside the lake, and you go through a gate into the Water Garden **D**. This was developed by Sir Philip Sassoon and after being neglected in the Second World War was restored and reopened in 1984. Retrace your steps to the fork **C** and turn right along a broad, gently ascending track through woodland, following London Loop waymarks again. Keep along the edge of the trees for a while before continuing through this delightful woodland again. Take the left-hand track at a fork, at a T-junction turn left, ignore a London Loop sign to the right and continue to another T-junction on the edge of the trees a few yards ahead **E**. Turn left,

passing an obelisk, and continue through the wood.

At the corner of the wood, follow the track to the left **F** and head gently downhill along the right inside edge of the wood – or alternatively along a parallel path along its right edge – and at the edge of the trees, turn right along the right edge of open grassland, by a hedge on the right, heading down to a T-junction. Turn right, here briefly rejoining the outward route and, at a London Loop post by a Trent Country Park noticeboard, turn right on to a path, by a hedge on the right.

At the corner of Oak Wood, turn left and keep alongside the right edge of a field up to a tarmac drive. Turn right alongside it and head towards the monument that was passed at the start of the walk and, just before reaching it, turn right along a tarmac path into the car park. ●

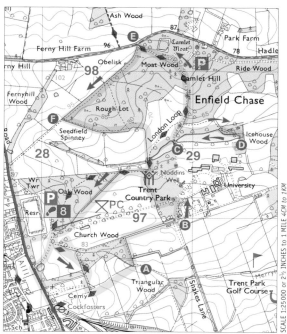

Osterley Park and the Grand Union Canal

		GPS waypoints
Start	Osterley Park	🖉 TQ 147 778
Distance	4½ miles (7.2km). Add 1 mile (1.6km) if coming from Osterley Station and pick up the walk at point **A**	**A** TQ 147 776 **B** TQ 150 789 **C** TQ 154 792 **D** TQ 137 794
Height gain	Negligible	**E** TQ 135 786
Approximate time	2 hours (3 hours from Osterley Station)	**F** TQ 143 784
Public transport	Underground to Osterley (Piccadilly line). Turn left, take the first turning on the left and at a T-junction keep ahead through the gates of the park. Walk along the main drive and look out for a metal kissing-gate on the right, where you join the main walk at point **A**	
Route terrain	Towpath, pavements and fields	
Ordnance Survey maps	Landranger 176 (West London), Explorer 161 (London South)	

This is a varied walk that leads from the expanses of Osterley Park to the towpath of the Grand Union Canal and on through part of the Brent River Park to Norwood Green. Historic interest ranges from Osterley Park House to Brunel's Three Bridges at Hanwell, which are a marvel of the Industrial Revolution. Its proximity to Heathrow Airport makes it a good walk for plane spotters.

🖉 From the car park, walk back along the broad, tree-lined drive and look out for a metal kissing-gate on the left **A**. Go through it, walk along a path enclosed between wire fences, go through another kissing-gate and follow the path around first a right and then a left bend. Where the path peters out, keep ahead along the left edge of a green, cross a track, take the left-hand path and continue to a road opposite the **Hare and Hounds** at Wyke Green.

Turn left along the busy road, pass under the M4 motorway and after about ½ mile, turn right beside a barrier on to a track **B** and immediately bear left to a kissing-gate. Go through, walk along a narrow enclosed path, by a high wire fence bordering a sports ground on the left, and at the corner of this fence, keep ahead through a metal gate and bear right to cross a railway line. Go through a kissing-gate and keep ahead to a road, continue along it and, after crossing a canal bridge, turn right through another kissing-gate and down steps to the towpath **C**. Turn sharp right to pass under the bridge and continue along the towpath of the Grand Union Canal for the next 1¼ miles, passing by the

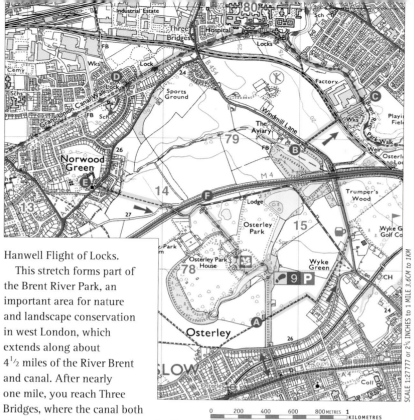

Hanwell Flight of Locks.

This stretch forms part of the Brent River Park, an important area for nature and landscape conservation in west London, which extends along about 4½ miles of the River Brent and canal. After nearly one mile, you reach Three Bridges, where the canal both crosses the railway and goes under the road. This intersection was designed by Brunel in 1855–6 and is unique in the way that three different modes of transport cross in one place.

After passing under the next bridge – No. 204 and painted white – go up steps **D**, turn right and right again to cross the bridge and keep ahead to a road, Melbury Avenue. Walk along it to a T-junction, turn left and, at the next T-junction, turn right along Tentelow Lane into Norwood Green. Turn left at the side of the **Plough**, at a public footpath sign 'Footpath Leading to St Mary's Avenue' **E**, walk along an enclosed path, cross a road and take the enclosed path opposite.

The path continues in a straight line across the middle of a large field, and on the far side climb steps and go through a kissing-gate on to a lane and keep ahead to cross a bridge over the

M4. The lane curves left. In front of gates turn right on to a tarmac track **F** and go through a gate to re-enter Osterley Park. Keep ahead along the straight, tree-lined track – later passing under an attractive avenue of trees – and bear right to go through a metal gate. The track passes in front of the house and curves left to keep alongside the Garden Lake on the right.

The redbrick Osterley Park House was originally an Elizabethan mansion built for Thomas Gresham, the founder of the Royal Exchange in the City of London, and then transformed by Robert Adam in 1761. In 1949 the house and its parkland were given to the National Trust.

Follow the track to the right around the end of the Garden Lake and, at a sign, turn left along a short stretch of path to return to the car park. ●

Wanstead Park

		GPS waypoints
Start	Wanstead Station	🚩 TQ 406 882
Distance	4½ miles (7.2km)	Ⓐ TQ 413 878
Height gain	Negligible	Ⓑ TQ 421 875
Approximate time	2 hours	Ⓒ TQ 418 871
Public transport	Underground to Wanstead (Central line)	Ⓓ TQ 416 874
		Ⓔ TQ 415 878
Route terrain	Lakeside paths, parkland	
Ordnance Survey maps	Landranger 177 (East London), Explorer 174 (Epping Forest & Lee Valley)	

This enchanting walk is through parkland where Wanstead Hall, a magnificent mansion, once stood which in its day was said to rival Hampton Court Palace. The route is laced in history and traces the path of the ornamental lakes, later crossing grassland to pass an 18th century garden building, The Temple.

🚩 Begin by turning left outside the station along tree-lined St Marys Avenue and keep ahead to the imposing church of St Mary the Virgin. There has been a church on this site from the 12th century and when the Earl of Leicester owned Wanstead Hall and invited Queen Elizabeth to stay, she worshipped here. The present church, built of white Portland stone to blend in with the style of the rebuilt Wanstead House, was consecrated in 1790.

Turn left at the church, along Overton Drive, and at the end of the road turn right into Warren Road. Just past some railings on the left, turn left Ⓐ between posts and head gently downhill. At a fork take the left-hand path and at the lake bear left to continue clockwise around it. The River Roding runs parallel to this for a short while on the left before the path curves right among the trees to a path junction Ⓑ. Here continue around the finger of one of the ornamental lakes.

Mansions at this time were built as showplaces and Wanstead's was no exception. The grounds were lavish and one of the ornamental lakes contained an island, canals were cut from the nearby River Roding and an expensive grotto was constructed with 'stalactites, crystals and looking glasses'. This is now but a ruin. Look out for herons here and during summer, the speckled wood butterfly.

Wanstead Park and its grand mansion attracted many royal visitors over the centuries but its demise came when its owner in 1812, Catherine Tylney Long and one of the country's richest heiresses, married a gambler, a nephew of the future Duke of Wellington.

Within 10 years the magnificent estate was squandered and it had to be sold in lots. Apparently, Catherine died at the age of 35 years of a broken heart.

At a crossing of paths bear right and at a fork bear left and keep ahead, until you reach another lake, Perch Pond, on

The Temple

your right.

Turn right Ⓒ and at a crossing of paths turn left. Continue to the next lake, Heronry Pond. Turn right, past a **white kiosk** that sells food and drinks during the summer months, along a wide path. At the next path junction turn right Ⓓ beside metal fencing surrounding The Temple, an 18th century listed garden building that is open at weekends and contains artefacts from the park.

At the next path junction turn left and soon the path runs alongside the lake. Keep ahead and turn left where you joined the lakeside walk Ⓔ. Retrace your steps to the start of the walk. ●

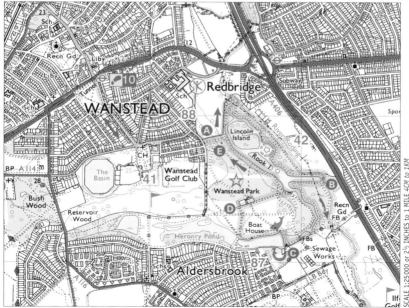

Totteridge and Mill Hill

		GPS waypoints
Start	Beside Sheepwash Pond, The Ridgeway	🖉 TQ 224 928
Distance	4½ miles (7.2km) [add 2 miles if walking from Mill Hill East underground station and joining the walk at point **Ⓐ**]	Ⓐ TQ 231 925 Ⓑ TQ 238 932 Ⓒ TQ 237 942 Ⓓ TQ 234 950
Height gain	325 feet (100m)	Ⓔ TQ 225 943 Ⓕ TQ 221 932
Approximate time	2 hours (3 hours if walking from the tube station)	
Public transport	Underground to Mill Hill East (Northern line), then bus no. 240 alighting at Three Hammers bus stop by Sheepwash Pond at the start, or St Vincents Lane, to join the walk at point **Ⓐ**	
Route features	Wild meadows, riverside paths and pavements	
Dog friendly	On a lead between points **Ⓔ** and **Ⓕ**	
Ordnance Survey maps	Lanranger 176 (West London), Explorer 173 (London North)	

The imposing buildings of Mill Hill School are soon left behind in this enjoyable and rural walk. There are plenty of stiles and kissing-gates to negotiate and a section of the route follows the Dollis Valley Greenwalk beside the Dollis brook. The walk also includes Totteridge Fields, an ancient grassland and one of the best examples of its kind in London.

🖉 Begin with your back to Sheepwash Pond and turn left to pass St Paul's Church, built by William Wilberforce. Keep ahead, passing the buildings of Mill Hill School, along The Ridgeway, an ancient trackway used by the Romans, Saxons and Normans. Back in the 1870s the headmaster of Mill Hill School, Sir James Murray, was asked to edit the *Oxford English Dictionary* and he later left Mill Hill for Oxford to devote more time to the project. It was so time-consuming it had taken him almost five years to reach the word 'ant'.

Turn left into St Vincents Lane **Ⓐ**, and at the gates to Belmont Racing Stables, go over a stile on the right, and keep along an enclosed path. Go over another stile and turn right, initially along a concrete path, and head diagonally right across a field. Cross a track and go over a stile to enter the field opposite. Here, head diagonally left to the middle of the row of trees, pass beside a waymarked fingerpost and maintain direction across the next field. In the field corner cross a wooden footbridge, keep along the left edge of the next field and turn left at the metal barrier. Just before the gates to Folly Farm turn right along an enclosed path beside a brook.

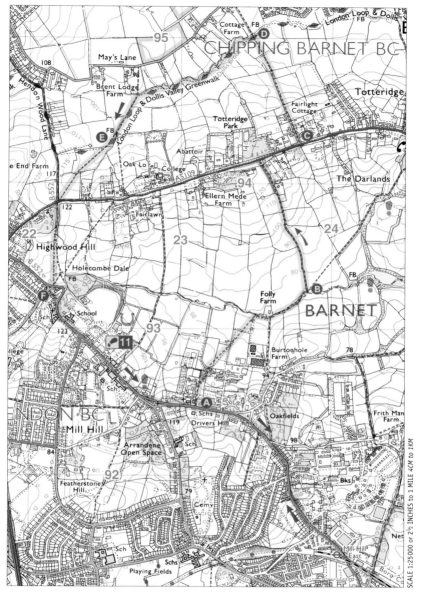

Turn left **B** at a public footpath sign to Long Ponds, Totteridge, beside a kissing-gate and follow the enclosed path between fields to go through a metal gate. Pass between two ponds and cross the road ahead. Turn right and keep ahead until you reach a green signpost to Mays Lane.

Here, turn left **C**, along Horseshoe

Lane and at the end, go over a stile beside a cottage. Continue along the left-hand edge of the next two fields and the right-hand edge of another and go over another stile. Keep ahead along a grassy path beside a row of pylons to a set of

An enclosed footpath near to Mill Hill

public footpath signs in front of a bridge.

Turn left **D**, before the bridge to follow the Dollis Valley Greenwalk. This riverside walk of 10 miles in length that stretches from Mill Hill to Hampstead provides many habitats for plants and wildlife. You may be lucky enough to spot kingfishers.

Go through a series of hedge gaps, plank footbridges and kissing-gates and then along an enclosed path, all the while keeping the Dollis Brook on your right. When you reach two plank footbridges beside a stile, keep ahead **E**, go up steps and bear left along the edge of a field.

Go through a hedge gap and then through a kissing-gate. Keep ahead (now leaving the London Loop path and the Dollis Valley Greenwalk), along a grassy path to pass a Totteridge Fields

information board by a footbridge. These ancient hay meadows criss-crossed by blackthorn and hawthorn hedgerows are ablaze with colour in the summer and provide a wonderful habitat for butterflies and birdlife.

Go through a kissing-gate to a road junction. Cross the road with care, bear right and look out for where you turn left at a public footpath sign to Mill Hill. Go through two kissing-gates and keep ahead along a tree-lined path which later descends along the right-hand field edge. Go through three further kissing-gates to reach the road. Cross this with care and continue along the road opposite, looking out for a green signpost to The Ridgeway. Turn left here **F**, and head uphill and then bear right, past the **Three Hammers pub** to return to the start of the walk. ●

Hampstead Heath

		GPS waypoints
Start	Hampstead Station	
Distance	4½ miles (7.2km)	🖋 TQ 264 858
Height gain	395 feet (120m)	**A** TQ 262 863
		B TQ 255 864
Approximate time	2½ hours	**C** TQ 260 869
Public transport	Underground to Hampstead	**D** TQ 265 871
	(Northern line)	**E** TQ 271 874
		F TQ 280 863
Route terrain	Heathland and woodland paths	**G** TQ 271 860
Ordnance Survey maps	Landranger 176 (West London), Explorer 173 (London North)	

The heathland, woodland and grassland of Hampstead Heath, a traditional and highly popular recreational area for Londoners, extends over 800 acres of north London and, unlike the royal parks of Central London, is a substantial wedge of surprisingly authentic and untamed countryside close to the city. It is also quite hilly and from its higher points, especially the 320 feet-high vantage point of Parliament Hill, there are superb and extensive views over London. Starting from Hampstead village, the walk does a circuit of the heath, passing three well-known pubs, and includes the elegant, 18th-century Kenwood House.

With narrow alleys and winding streets, small squares and picturesque cottages, Hampstead retains its village-like atmosphere more perhaps than any other area of London. In the 18th century it became a fashionable spa, and a number of handsome houses date from that period. Its almost rural, hilltop position on the edge of the heath – out of the city but not too far away – has long made Hampstead a desirable place to live.

🖋 Turn right out of the station, walk up Heath Street to the edge of the heath and keep ahead towards **Jack Straw's Castle**, an 18th-century inn, though almost totally rebuilt in the 1960s. It is named after one of the leaders of the Peasants' Revolt, who is

alleged to have gathered together a mob near here in 1381. Just after passing Whitestone Pond on the left – and before reaching the inn – turn left **A** on to a path across West Heath. Head downhill through woodland into a dip and, before emerging on to a road, bear right to continue along the left edge of the heath. The path later continues beside West Heath Road to a broad track.

Turn right **B** along this track (Sandy Road), pass to the left of a pond called the Leg of Mutton and head gently uphill to reach a tarmac drive. Continue along it, going round a left bend, to a road opposite the **Old Bull and Bush**, another old pub, made famous in a Victorian music-hall song. Turn right, almost immediately turn left along

Hampstead Heath – around 790 acres of hills and valleys rising to 440 feet

North End **C** and, where the road ends, pass beside a barrier and continue along a track through the woodland of Sandy Heath. Keep on the main, broad track all the time, which bears left and continues to a road. About 100 yds to the left is the **Spaniards Inn**, the third of the trio of traditional heath pubs, a mainly 18th-century building. It claims to date back to 1585 and to have been frequented by Dick Turpin.

Turn right along Spaniards Inn Road and after a few yards turn left through a gate on to an enclosed path **D**. Take the left-hand, downhill path at a fork, which curves left through the trees to another fork. Again take the left-hand path, which continues down to reach a clear, well-surfaced track at a junction.

Continue along the track straight ahead, which meanders across open grassland, bearing right to go through a gate to a T-junction.

Turn left on to a broad track, which bears right to continue across the terrace in front of Kenwood House. This elegant 18th-century mansion, designed by Robert Adam for the Earl of Mansfield, was bequeathed to the nation in 1927 by Edward Guinness, Earl of Iveagh. The 'Iveagh Bequest' included the grounds, a popular venue for outdoor concerts in the summer, and his superb collection of paintings.

At a fork at the end of the terrace, take the right-hand track **E**, which curves right and descends, passing to the left of a lake. Keep ahead through woodland, by a wire fence on the right, and go through a metal gate to a crossway on the edge of open heathland again. Continue along the tarmac track in front, take the left-hand path at a fork and pass through a belt of trees to a track. Keep ahead along a grassy path, heading gently uphill, and at a fork just over the slight rise take the left-hand path, which descends to a tarmac path.

Turn left and follow it along the right edge of two of the series of Highgate Ponds; the path soon broadens out into a wide track. At a junction by the end of the last pond, turn sharp right **F** on to a gently ascending path. At the next junction continue along the right-hand path and follow it up to the top of Parliament Hill. Despite a modest height of 320 ft, the views, both the nearer ones across to Hampstead and Highgate villages and the wider ones over London, are outstanding. A viewfinder

identifies all the places that can be seen from here in clear conditions.

Keep ahead past the viewfinder, descending towards woodland, and continue through the trees. The path continues to descend and crosses a causeway between two of the Hampstead Ponds. Head uphill for about 50 yds and turn sharp right **G** on to a path along the right edge of grassland, later entering woodland and climbing steps to reach a track. This is the Boundary Path, and you turn left along this beautiful, tree-lined track to emerge on to East Heath Road.

Turn right uphill, turn left at a blue footpath signpost to Christ Church and pass to the right of the church. Turn right along Elm Row to a T-junction and turn left down Heath Street to the start. ●

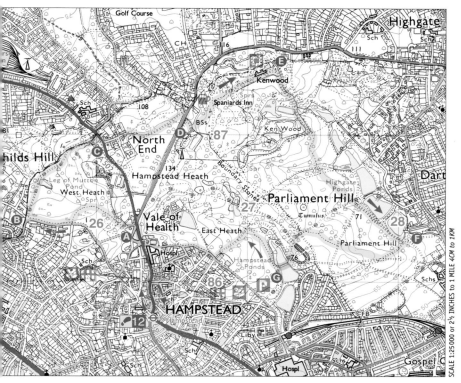

SCALE 1:25000 or 2½ INCHES to 1 MILE 4CM to 1KM

Banstead Wood and Park Downs

		GPS waypoints
Start	Chipstead	
Distance	4½ miles (7.2km). Add ½ mile (800m) if coming from Chipstead Station	🥾 TQ 273 583 Ⓐ TQ 259 575 Ⓑ TQ 250 575 Ⓒ TQ 249 579 Ⓓ TQ 256 588 Ⓔ TQ 270 586
Height gain	325 feet (100m)	
Approximate time	2½ hours	
Parking	Holly Lane car park	
Public transport	Trains from London (Victoria) to Chipstead. Turn left out of the station and follow a road to the right down to the main road. Turn left, take the first turning on the right – Lower Park Road – and the car park is about 100 yds along on the left	
Route terrain	Woodland paths and downland tracks	
Ordnance Survey maps	Landranger 187 (Dorking & Reigate), Explorer 146 (Dorking, Box Hill & Reigate)	

There is a surprisingly remote feel on parts of this well-waymarked walk, despite being almost enveloped by suburban Surrey and not far from the M25. The route begins by following the edge of Banstead Wood, an ancient woodland with a wide range of animal and plant species. On this stretch there are fine views over the Chipstead Valley. It then heads across more open country to continue through the attractive woodland and chalk downland of Park Downs, which is an area of common land managed by a board of conservators.

🥾 With your back to the road, make for the top left corner of the car park and go through a kissing-gate. Take the path ahead and, at a fingerpost by a junction of paths and tracks, follow a track into the woodland, in the direction of a public footpath sign to Perrotts Farm. At the next footpath sign a few yards ahead, bear left to continue along the left edge of Banstead Wood, following the signs for the Banstead Country Walk. The path heads uphill along the edge of the wood; to the left the views over the Chipstead Valley are most attractive.

At a fork by a footpath sign, keep ahead, in the 'Summer Route' direction, along a path that contours along a wooded hillside. Continue along the right edge of trees, in the Fames Rough direction, cross a track and keep ahead to re-enter the wood, following the regular Banstead Country Walk signs all the while. The path bears right and

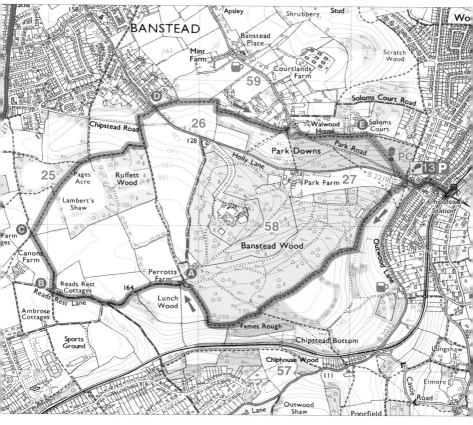

ascends gently to a T-junction. Turn left, in the 'Main Route' direction, then keep ahead at the next footpath sign and the path curves right to head up to a stile.

Climb the stile, continue along the left edge of the wood towards a farm and climb another stile in the field corner Ⓐ. Turn left on to a track, at a public bridleway sign to Burgh Heath, pass in front of the farmhouse and continue along the broad track that bends right towards cottages. At a crossing of tracks just beyond the cottages – where there is a public footpath sign, turn right Ⓑ through a gate and keep ahead along a track to a stile beside a gate.

Climb the stile, continue along the left edge of a field and at a public footpath sign to Holly Lane Ⓒ turn diagonally right across the field towards trees. Go through a kissing-gate on the far side, continue through the trees and then bear left along the left edge of a field to go through another kissing-gate. Walk along the right, inside edge of woodland, bear right on joining another path and keep ahead along the left edge of Ruffett Wood, descending to a T-junction.

Turn left, climb a stile in the field corner and keep ahead through trees, curving right to emerge on to a road Ⓓ. Cross over and walk along the left edge of a field. Follow the field edge to the right and, at a footpath post, turn left. Continue along an attractive, tree-lined path and at a fork by a Banstead Common information board, take the left-hand path, which heads over Park Downs along the edge of the trees.

Keep ahead, in the Park Road direction, cross a lane and take the path ahead through more delightful woodland.

Continue along the left-hand path and look out for a footpath post, where you turn right **E** on to a path that winds downhill through the trees to emerge into a more open, grassy area. Bear left, immediately turn right, by a Banstead Country Walk sign, and the path continues down to Holly Lane opposite the car park. ●

A lane through Park Downs

Marden Park Woods

			GPS waypoints
Start	Woldingham Station		TQ 359 563
Distance	4½ miles (7.2km). Shorter version 2½ miles (4km)		Ⓐ TQ 365 555
Height gain	410 feet (125m)		Ⓑ TQ 366 548
Approximate time	2½ hours (1 hour for the shorter walk)		Ⓒ TQ 370 549
Parking	Woldingham Station		Ⓓ TQ 373 540
Public transport	Trains from London (Victoria) to Woldingham		Ⓔ TQ 368 536
Route terrain	Woodland paths and tracks		Ⓕ TQ 362 548
Dog friendly	Sheep may be grazing		
Ordnance Survey maps	Landranger 187 (Dorking & Reigate), Explorer 146 (Dorking, Box Hill & Reigate)		

*Much of this well-waymarked walk is through the attractive
Marden Park Woods, from where there are fine views over the
Marden Valley and rolling chalk downland. A short stretch of the
North Downs Way is used, and from here you look southwards
across the well-wooded ridges and valleys of the Weald. There is
also the chance to visit the highest, and certainly one of the
smallest, churches in Surrey.*

Turn right out of the station car park along Church Road, which keeps parallel to the railway line. The road becomes a rough track, and you continue along it as far as a public footpath sign 'Woldingham Countryside walk', just before reaching woodland Ⓐ. Turn right down to a stile, climb it and turn left on to an enclosed path above a steep cutting. The path turns right to cross the railway line and continues to another stile. Climb it, turn left and head steadily uphill through the trees to reach a T-junction Ⓑ.

If doing the short walk, turn right and head downhill, still through woodland, to a

St Agathas Church

The woodland of Marden Park

junction of tracks **F**, *where you turn right again, in the Woldingham Station direction, to rejoin the full walk.*

For the full walk, turn left uphill, take the left-hand track at a fork and continue up to a kissing-gate on the right that admits you to Great Church Wood **C**. A brief detour ahead leads to the attractive, early-19th-century St Agatha's Church. At 775 ft, this is the highest church in Surrey; it may also possibly be the smallest.

The route continues, via the kissing-gate, along a path through Great Church Wood, which like much of Marden Park Woods is now owned by the Woodland Trust. The path ahead curves downhill and eventually descends a flight of steps to a track. Turn left, head uphill through Marden Park Wood, go through a gate and on through South Hawke car park to a lane. Turn right, almost immediately turn left down steps and, at a T-junction, turn right along a path, here joining the North Downs Way **D**. On this section of the route, gaps in the trees on the left reveal grand and extensive views across the Weald, but the noise from the M25 immediately below is inescapable. Follow the regular North Downs Way signs, curving right and then turning left, and the tree-lined path later runs parallel to the lane and eventually emerges on to it. Walk along the lane and turn right through a gate **E** at a Woodland Trust notice, into another part of Marden Park Wood.

The track bears left, later narrows to a path and continues through this beautiful area of woodland, following the regular 'Woldingham Countryside Walk' waymarks. Climb a stile to emerge from the trees, head downhill along the left edge of the wood and, at the bottom, climb another stile on to a tarmac drive.

Continue, passing between the school buildings on the left and a cemetery on the right, and the tarmac drive becomes a rough track that heads uphill between embankments to a junction of tracks **F**.

Keep ahead – here rejoining the short walk – in the Woldingham Station direction along an enclosed, tree- and hedge-lined track, enjoying the views to the left over the beautiful and secluded Marden Valley. The track descends to a farm. Keep ahead. The track becomes a tarmac one that bends right and crosses the railway line to a T-junction. Turn left, rejoining the outward route, and follow Church Road back to the start. ●

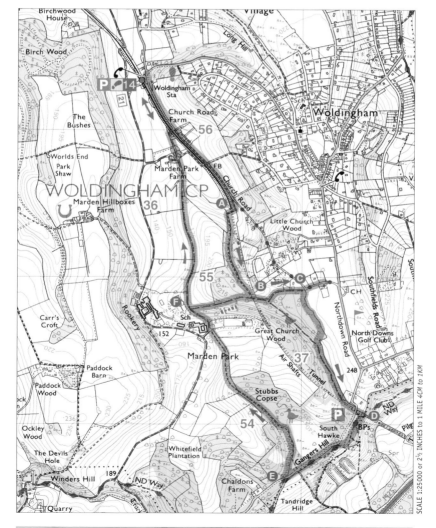

Blackheath and Greenwich Park

		GPS waypoints
Start	Blackheath Station	
Distance	5 miles (8km)	TQ 396 760
Height gain	165 feet (50m)	Ⓐ TQ 392 768
		Ⓑ TQ 389 772
Approximate time	2½ hours	Ⓒ TQ 382 779
Parking	Blackheath Station (there are	Ⓓ TQ 383 783
	other car parks in Blackheath)	Ⓔ TQ 386 780
Public transport	Trains from London (Charing Cross)	Ⓕ TQ 395 772
	to Blackheath	
Route terrain	Parkland	
Ordnance Survey maps	Landranger 177 (East London),	
	Explorer 162 (Greenwich & Gravesend)	

The first and last parts of the walk are across Blackheath; most of the remainder is a circuit of Greenwich Park, passing the Old Royal Observatory, National Maritime Museum and Royal Naval College buildings. From the higher points in the park, the superb views include Greenwich below and the great sweep of the River Thames, with St Paul's Cathedral, Canary Wharf and the O2 Arena on the skyline. The route also includes a walk under the Greenwich Foot Tunnel to Island Gardens on the Isle of Dogs in order to experience the classic view of Greenwich, looking back across the river to the complex of buildings, with the park rising behind them.

Turn left out of the station, take the right-hand road at a fork and take the first turning on the left, Montpelier Vale, up to the heath. Because of its location astride the main approach to London from Dover and the continent, Blackheath has witnessed a number of stirring national events over the centuries. Wat Tyler and his rebels assembled here to meet Richard II during the Peasants' Revolt in 1381. A later rebel force, led by Jack Cade, also met here in 1450. Henry VII defeated Cornish rebels on the heath in 1497.

Henry V was welcomed here in 1415 after his triumph at Agincourt, and Charles II entered his capital from Blackheath at the Restoration of the Monarchy in 1660.

Cross a road and continue along All Saints' Drive, passing to the left of All Saints Church. Keep ahead along a gravel path across the heath, take the right-hand path at a fork and continue to a road. Bear right along it to cross a road, keep ahead to cross another one and continue along Duke Humphrey Road. After crossing another road, you

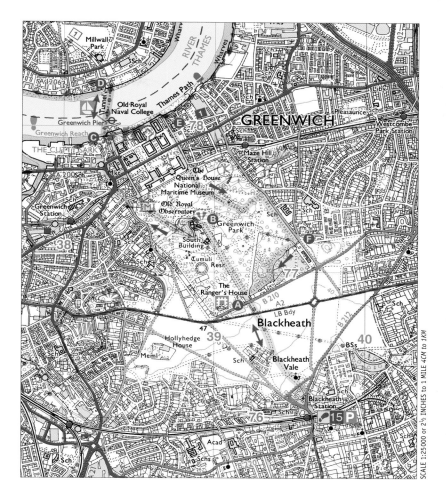

enter Greenwich Park by Blackheath Gate **A**. This is the oldest of the royal parks, enclosed by Humphrey Duke of Gloucester, uncle of Henry VI, in 1433.

Keep straight ahead along a tree-lined road to the Old Royal Observatory and the statue to General Wolfe **B**. From here the view over Greenwich, the River Thames, the Millennium Dome and the London skyline is magnificent. Charles II founded the Royal Observatory in 1675 for the study of astronomy and marine navigation. Later the Prime Meridian Line, 0° longitude, was positioned here, giving visitors the unusual experience of being able to stand with one foot in

the western hemisphere and the other in the eastern hemisphere. The Royal Observatory buildings are now part of the National Maritime Museum.

At a fork just beyond the statue, take the left-hand path – going through a metal gate and not down the steps – which crosses the Greenwich Meridian Line, curves left in front of the observatory and descends to a park road. Turn right downhill, leave the park by St Mary's Gate and keep ahead along King William Walk into Greenwich. Turn left along Nelson

Road to St Alfege's Church, built by Hawksmoor in 1714 and restored after bomb damage in the Second World War, and turn right along Greenwich Church Street. Turn right again into College Approach and, in front of the gates of the Royal Naval College, turn left to Greenwich Pier and the *Cutty Sark* **C**. This grand old sailing ship was the last and fastest of the tea-clippers.

Turn left by the pier to a circular, domed brick building. This is the entrance to the Greenwich Foot Tunnel, opened in 1902, which takes you under the Thames to emerge at Island Gardens. Turn right for the classic view across the river at Greenwich **D**. Apart from the Old Royal Observatory on the hill, this uniquely imposing and grandiose complex of Classical buildings comprises the Royal Naval College, the Queen's House and the National Maritime Museum. Its building history and variety of roles is quite complicated. The original medieval manor house was rebuilt by Henry VII, and it was in this palace, called Placentia, that Henry VIII, Mary I and Elizabeth I were all born. In the early 17th century, Inigo Jones was commissioned to build the Queen's House, regarded as the first Classical building in England, for the wife of James I, although it was completed for Henrietta Maria, Charles I's wife. In the 1660s, Charles II demolished the Tudor palace and began the construction of a new one but the site of this was later donated by Mary II as a hospital for seamen. Wren was the architect for this Royal Naval Hospital but it was not completed until long after his death. In 1873 it changed its role to become the Royal Naval College, and the Queen's House and adjoining buildings became the National Maritime Museum in 1933. At present the future of the college is again in doubt as the Ministry of Defence no longer need it and are about to vacate the buildings.

Retrace your steps under the Thames to Greenwich and turn left alongside the river, following Thames Path signs. Pass in front of the Royal Naval College, turn right, between the college on your right and the **Trafalgar Tavern**, a traditional riverside pub, on your left, and take the first turning on the left **E** for a short detour along the Thames Path to a garden area in front of Trinity Hospital, an almshouse founded in 1613. The hospital is dwarfed by the adjacent power station.

Return to the **Trafalgar Tavern**, turn left to continue along Park Row, cross the main road and keep ahead alongside the Queen's House to re-enter the park. Take the broad path ahead, passing to the right of a children's boating pool, and at a junction of paths, bear left, in the 'Flower Garden and Deer Enclosure' direction, along another broad, tree-lined path. Head uphill, passing to the right of a mound and, at a crossway, turn left on to a narrower path, which continues up to Maze Hill Gate. The brick-built house just to the left on the other side of the road is Vanbrugh Castle, designed by Vanbrugh and his home from 1719 to 1726.

Do not go through the gate but turn right to follow a path alongside the park wall to a junction of paths by Vanbrugh Park Gate **F**. At this junction, turn half-right and enter the flower garden through a metal gate. Keep ahead to a T-junction in front of a pond. The deer park is over to the left. Turn left and the path curves right and follows the perimeter of the pond. Go through a metal gate on to the main park road.

Turn left through Blackheath Gate **A**, here picking up the outward route, and retrace your steps to the start. ●

Hainault Forest

		GPS waypoints
Start	Hainault Forest Country Park, first car park near the café	 🖉 TQ 476 926 Ⓐ TQ 480 930 Ⓑ TQ 479 938
Distance	5 miles (8km). Add 3½ miles (5.6km) if coming from Grange Hill Station and pick up the walk at point Ⓖ	Ⓒ TQ 487 945 Ⓓ TQ 479 951 Ⓔ TQ 477 944 Ⓕ TQ 478 936
Height gain	280 feet (85m)	Ⓖ TQ 473 926
Approximate time	2½ hours (4 hours from Grange Hill Station)	
Parking	Hainault Forest Country Park	
Public transport	Underground to Grange Hill (Central line). Turn right along Manor Road, turn right at traffic lights by the Maypole pub and at the next set of traffic lights, turn left through a fence gap into the country park and follow a path to the lake, where you join the main route at point Ⓖ	
Route terrain	Parkland and quiet country lanes	
Ordnance Survey maps	Landranger 177 (East London), Explorer 174 (Epping Forest & Lee Valley)	

Although a smaller remnant of the ancient Forest of Essex than Epping, Hainault Forest is nevertheless a superb remnant with expanses of open grassland combined with some outstandingly beautiful woodland. Considering that the forest is on the doorstep of north-east London – Canary Wharf tower is visible at times – the views over the Essex countryside from its eastern and northern fringes are surprisingly peaceful and rural. This is a figure-of-eight walk, with a pub approximately halfway round.

Hainault Forest, originally part of the vast forest of Essex, was held by the abbots of Barking until the dissolution of the monasteries, when it was acquired by Henry VIII. It remained Crown property until 1851, after which the forest was enclosed and much of it felled. What remained was bought by London County Council in 1903 as a recreation area, and it has subsequently become a popular country park.

🖉 Start by facing the **café** and turn

left along the tarmac drive, passing to the left of Foxburrows Farm, now a rare breeds centre, and the buildings of the Country Park Office. Where the drive ends in front of the gates of a golf course, turn left Ⓐ along a tree-lined path that bears slightly right and heads gently uphill into woodland. At a junction of paths by a Hainault Forest Country Park notice, keep ahead into the trees and, after about 75 yds, turn right at the crossways marked by a

A pathway through Hainault Forest

'Camelot car park' post **B**.

Continue through beautiful woodland, at a fork take the left-hand path, heading gently downhill to cross a tiny brook, and eventually you go through a kissing-gate to a T-junction near the edge of the forest. Turn right uphill, passing to the right of houses, to a footpath post **C**. At this point a brief detour ahead leads to a fine view over the tranquil and gently rolling Essex countryside.

At the footpath post, turn left to climb a stile and walk along a grassy path enclosed between wire fences to continue gently uphill along the right edge of a field and in the top corner, cross a plank footbridge over a ditch on to a road. Turn left and at a junction turn right along New Road, signposted to Abridge, through Lambourne End. Where the road bends right, turn left over a stile **D** at a public footpath sign, bear right downhill along the right edge of a field. Climb a stile, continue downhill and climb another stile on to a lane.

Turn left and follow the undulating

lane to a T-junction beside the **Miller & Carter pub** 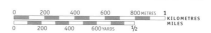. Cross over, keep ahead through a car park and pass beside a barrier to re-enter the Country Park. Continue through more delightful woodland to the crossway passed earlier **B** and keep ahead for about 75 yds – briefly joining the outward route. On emerging from the trees, turn right. Immediately take the left-hand path at a fork, go over a stile and turn left at a white-waymarked post **F**.

Turn right at a crossway, and the path heads gently downhill, winding along the left, inside edge of woodland. From here there are fine views across the open grassland to the left, with the tower of Canary Wharf visible on the horizon. Look out for a crossing of paths – just before crossing a brook – where you turn left. Take the right-hand path at a fork and continue along the right edge of the lake for a pleasant finale to the walk, following the curve of the lake round to the left **G**.

Walkers returning to Grange Hill turn right here to pick up the outward route and retrace their steps to the station.

The path heads back along the other side of the lake and bends right to return to the start. ●

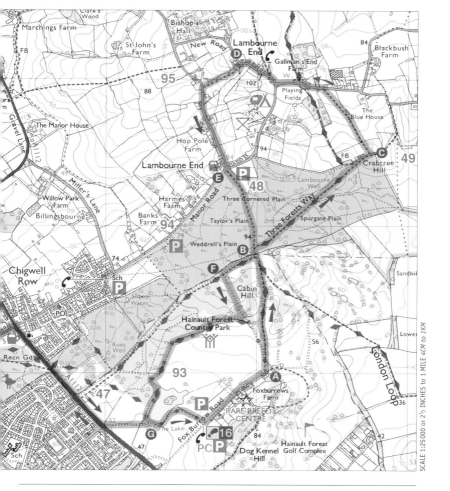

Little Venice, Regent's Park and Primrose Hill

		GPS waypoints
Start	Little Venice	✎ TQ 261 818
Distance	5½ miles (8.9km). Shorter version 5 miles (8km)	Ⓐ TQ 265 821
		Ⓑ TQ 273 831
		Ⓒ TQ 279 828
Height gain	130 feet (40m)	Ⓓ TQ 283 826
Approximate time	2½ hours (2 hours for shorter walk)	Ⓔ TQ 286 829
		Ⓕ TQ 282 836
Public transport	Underground to Warwick Avenue (Bakerloo line). Walk along Warwick Avenue to the crossroads, and Little Venice is to the right	Ⓖ TQ 276 839
		Ⓗ TQ 277 834
Route terrain	Towpath and parkland	
Ordnance Survey maps	Landranger 176 (West London), Explorer 173 (London North)	

From the canal basin at Little Venice, the walk proceeds beside an attractive stretch of the Regent's Canal to Regent's Park. This is followed by a circuit of this superb park, including a visit to the ornamental Queen Mary's Gardens. A short detour to the summit of Primrose Hill provides a grand panoramic view over London. The shorter walk omits this detour and returns directly to Little Venice along the canal.

Little Venice, the nickname given to the canal basin just to the north of Paddington Station, is the starting point of both the Grand Union and Regent's canals. It is a most attractive area, with colourful gardens and leafy roads, lined with handsome and dignified Victorian houses along the canal banks. The Regent's Canal was opened in 1820 and runs from here to Limehouse Basin, completing the link between Birmingham and the Thames.

✎ Start by walking along Blomfield Road, with the canal on the right, cross Warwick Avenue and continue along the tree-lined left bank of the canal up to Edgware Road Ⓐ. At this point the

Regent's Canal disappears into the Maida Vale tunnel. Keep ahead along Aberdeen Place and look out for a blue plaque on a house where Guy Gibson, who led the Dambusters raid, lived. Where the road turns left, take the path in front and descend iron steps to rejoin the canal. Walk along the towpath, going first under a tunnel and then under foot, rail and road bridges in quick succession. The greenery of Regent's Park can be seen over to the right.

After passing under the next bridge (Charlbert Bridge) Ⓑ, turn left up a path, turn sharp left and then left again to cross the bridge, cross a road and go through Charlbert Bridge Gate into

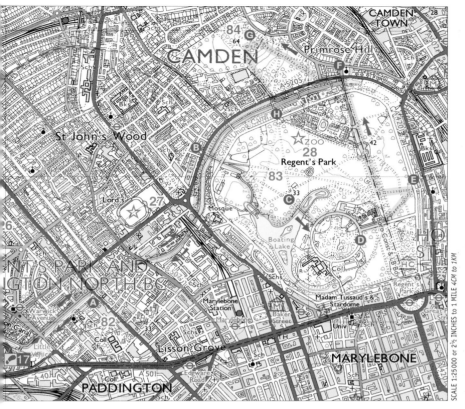

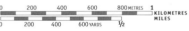

Regent's Park. In the Middle Ages this area was part of the Forest of Middlesex but in the 16th century it was acquired by Henry VIII, who converted it into the royal hunting ground of Marylebone Park. It assumed its present form in the early 19th century when John Nash transformed this part of London and surrounded the park with elegant terraces. London Zoo occupies part of the north side of the park, and to the west is the London Mosque.

Take the right-hand path at a fork and at the next fork take the right-hand path again to reach the end of the boating lake. Continue along the left edge of the lake as it curves left, turn right ● to cross a footbridge over it and keep ahead through Longbridge Gate on to the Inner Circle. This road encircles the Inner Park or Queen

Mary's Gardens. Turn left and follow the curve of the circle to the right to Chester Road Gate ●, where you can enter the colourful and attractive Queen Mary's Gardens, predominantly a rose garden set amid a small ornamental lake.

Returning to the Chester Road Gate, keep ahead along Chester Road and, at a pedestrian crossing, turn left into Broad Walk, a wide, straight, tree-lined drive. Immediately turn right off it on to a path that bears left to Cumberland Gate ● in order to take a look at Cumberland Terrace – across the road on the left – probably the most impressive of the Regency terraces built around the park by Nash. Re-enter the park and take the path to the right of your previous path to rejoin the Broad Walk. Turn right along it, later keeping along the right edge of London Zoo, go through a gate to leave the park and cross first a road and then the canal bridge to reach another road, Prince Albert Road **F**.

If you wish to omit the detour to Primrose Hill, turn right, then sharp right, at a footpath sign, to descend to the canal towpath and keep along it, picking up the full walk at point **H**.

For the full walk, turn left to the corner of Albert Terrace, where you cross the road to enter Primrose Hill, acquired as an extension to Regent's Park in 1841. At a fork take the right-hand path, which heads gently uphill and curves left to the viewfinder at the top **G**. Although only 219 ft high, the views over London are superb and take in many major landmarks, including the dome of St Paul's and, inevitably, Canary Wharf tower.

Keep ahead past the viewfinder along a path that curves left downhill to join a straight path and continue along it to emerge on to Prince Albert Road again. Turn right and then first left at a ZSL building and head towards the canal. Just before reaching the bridge, turn right onto a hedge-lined path, which turns sharp left and then sharp right on to the towpath **H**. Here you pick up the outward route and retrace your steps to the start. ●

Primrose Hill view

Hampton Court and Bushy parks

		GPS waypoints
Start	Hampton Court Station on south side of Hampton Court Bridge	🖉 TQ 153 684
Distance	5½ miles (8.9km) or via embankment between April – October 6¼ miles (10km)	**Ⓐ** TQ 155 686
		Ⓑ TQ 159 683
		Ⓒ TQ 174 679
Height gain	Negligible	**Ⓓ** TQ 174 693
Approximate time	2½ hours	**Ⓔ** TQ 170 697
Parking	Hampton Court Station	**Ⓕ** TQ 159 698
Public transport	Trains from London (Waterloo) to Hampton Court	
Route terrain	Thames side paths and parkland	
Dog friendly	Dogs not allowed in the formal gardens of Hampton Court and Bushey Park contains deer	
Ordnance Survey maps	Landranger 176 (West London), Explorer 161 (London South)	

Inevitably the chief focal point of the walk is the magnificent Hampton Court Palace, the nearest England has to Versailles, and there are some memorable views of it on the first part of the route. From the palace and its ornamental gardens, the walk heads across Hampton Court Park to the banks of the River Thames and then follows the river to Kingston Bridge. The return to Hampton Court is across the wide and open expanses of the adjacent Bushy Park. Deer are likely to be seen in both parks.

Note: There is an entrance fee to see the formal gardens but note there is no access from the formal gardens to Home Park from 1 April – 30 September. If you are following the route between these dates you can pick up the embankment path to the right of Hampton Court Palace. Here, turn left and continue to **Ⓒ**.

🖉 Start by crossing Hampton Court Bridge, turn right through the gates of the palace and walk along a broad drive, parallel to the river. Hampton Court Palace is really two palaces in one: the original redbrick Tudor palace, built by Cardinal Wolsey and altered by Henry VIII, and the elegant late 17th-century extension designed by Wren for William III and Mary II. The contrast between the two halves is quite striking.

The palace was built by Wolsey in 1514 and given to Henry VIII in 1525 in a desperate but unsuccessful attempt to keep in favour with the King. It became

Hampton Court Palace

Henry's favourite residence. He built the Great Hall, noted for its superb hammer-beam roof, two of his marriages took place here, and his third wife, Jane Seymour, died in the palace in 1537 shortly after giving birth to the future Edward VI. Over a century later, following the accession to the throne of William III and Mary II in 1689, Wren was entrusted with building an extension that would turn Hampton Court into an English Versailles. William and Mary were also responsible for the ornamental gardens; the Maze – a popular attraction with visitors – was created a little later in the reign of Queen Anne.

Turn left in front of Wolsey's Great Gatehouse, go under an arch, keep ahead along the right edge of gardens and turn right through a gate **A**. Continue along a straight path, sign-posted 'Vine and Toilets', go through a gate and turn right to walk along the east front of the palace, part of Wren's 17th-century extension. Turn left towards a fountain, and beyond that is the start of the Long Water, created for

Charles II shortly after the Restoration, possibly as a reminder of Holland, where he had spent his exile. At a statue just in front of the lake, turn right, turn left to cross a footbridge **B** and go through wrought-iron gates into the park.

The path bears left to join a tarmac track. Continue along it, turning left by farm buildings and bending right to continue alongside Long Water. Where the lake ends, keep ahead at a crossing of tracks and shortly bear right off the track along a grassy path that skirts the left edge of Rick Pond and continues to a metal gate in a fence. Go through, walk along a fence-lined path and go through another metal gate to the River Thames at River Raven Ait (island) **C**.

Turn left on to the riverside path – it later becomes a wide tarmac track – and follow it for ¾ mile to Kingston Bridge. At the bridge, turn left into Hampton Wick, follow the road to the left and turn right into Church Grove **D**, signposted to Teddington. The road bears left and, where it bends right, turn left through a metal gate to enter Bushy Park **E**. The tarmac path, Cobbler's Path, which you take across the park, gets its name from a local shoemaker, Timothy Bennet, who threatened court action against the Earl of Halifax, the park ranger, when he closed the path in 1752. Halifax backed down, and the path has remained a public right of way ever since. At the entrance to the park is a memorial to Timothy Bennet.

After crossing a narrow stream, bear left and continue along the path until you reach a fence on the left. Bear left on to a grassy path, which follows the curve of the fence round to the left to join a tarmac path by a house. Take the second – not the first – path on the right, which bears slightly left to the Chestnut Avenue **F**. This was planned

by Wren as a grand approach to a new northern façade to Hampton Court Palace, which was never built. Turn left beside the avenue, continue past the imposing Diana Fountain and leave the park by the Hampton Court Gate.

Go through the Lion Gate opposite to re-enter Hampton Court Park and, at a meeting of paths ahead, take the one to the right, passing to the left of the Maze. Turn left at a T-junction in front of the tearoom and at a crossing of paths rejoin the outward route to retrace your steps to the start. ●

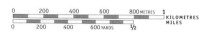

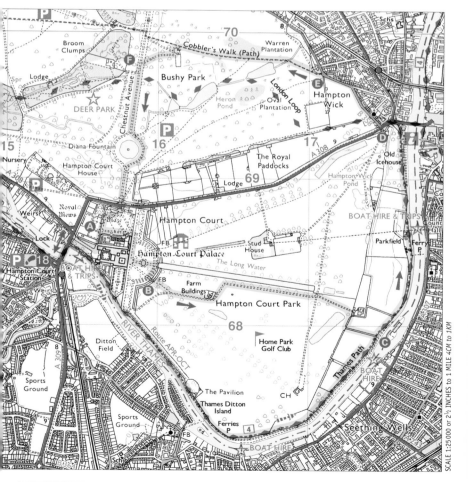

Ruislip Woods and Lido

		GPS waypoints	
Start	Ruislip Lido	🖉	TQ 087 892
Distance	5½ miles (8.9km). Add 1¼ miles (2km) if coming from Ruislip Manor Station and pick up the walk at point **G**	**A**	TQ 084 896
		B	TQ 082 903
		C	TQ 088 902
		D	TQ 091 894
Height gain	230 feet (70m)	**E**	TQ 093 887
Approximate time	3 hours (3½ hours from Ruislip Manor Station)	**F**	TQ 100 883
		G	TQ 096 881
Parking	Ruislip Lido	**H**	TQ 090 880
Public transport	Underground to Ruislip Manor (Metropolitan line). Turn right and join the main route just after crossing the bridge over the River Pinn at point **G**		
Route terrain	Woodland and meadows		
Ordnance Survey maps	Landranger 176 (West London), Explorers 172 (Chiltern Hills East) and 173 (London North)		

Much of this route is through the attractive woodlands, remnants of the old Forest of Middlesex, that lie between Ruislip and Northwood, with a foray into suburban Ruislip for a walk across meadows bordering the little River Pinn. Towards the end come grand views across Ruislip Lido. You need to take careful heed of the route directions through Ruislip Woods as most of the paths are not waymarked.

🖉 From the car park entrance by the **Waters Edge pub**, go through a gate, at a Hillingdon Trail waymark, and walk along a well-constructed path across meadowland. At the next Hillingdon Trail sign, bear left across the grass and go through a gate into Copse Wood.

The path curves left at a Hillingdon Trail footpath post but at the next post turn right **A** to leave the Hillingdon Trail and continue gently uphill through this delightful area of woodland. Turn right at a T-junction, almost immediately turn left and keep in a straight line, heading gently downhill to pass through a barrier to a T-junction on the edge of the wood **B**. Turn right to emerge on to the end of a road and in 400 yds turn right on to a path that re-enters the wood.

Look out for a path on the left that winds through the trees down to a fence and kissing-gate. Do not go through the gate but turn left on to a fence-lined path that keeps along the right, inside edge of the wood. Keep ahead at a crossway, bear left and cross a small brook to emerge on to the edge of a golf course. Turn right **C** along a path that winds along the left, inside edge of the trees, follows the edge of the trees to the left and continues along the right edge of the golf course.

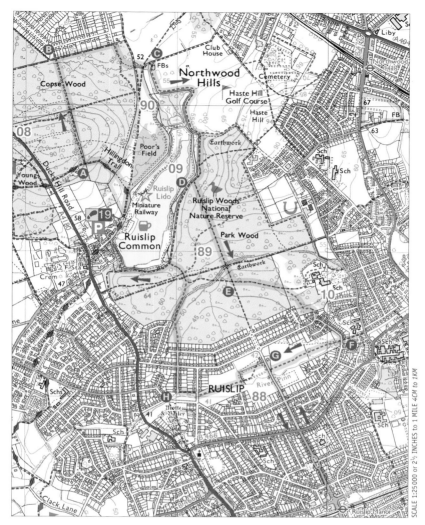

SCALE 1:25 000 or 2½ INCHES to 1 MILE 4CM to 1KM

0	200	400	600	800 METRES	1
					KILOMETRES
					MILES
0	200	400	600 YARDS	½	

Turn sharp right to cross a footbridge over a brook, continue along the left edge of woodland, by a high wire fence on the right, bear left and then turn right to follow the path into Park Wood. Continue in a more or less straight line through the wood and soon you see a miniature railway line beyond a wire fence on the right. Just after the path bears slightly right, turn left **D** to continue past a row of posts along a clear, straight, steadily ascending path. The path later levels off and then gently descends to a major junction of paths

and tracks. Cross a small brook, keep ahead gently uphill again and after about 100 yds another path comes in from the right. At this point turn left **E** to pick up a path and follow it to the edge of the trees.

Bear right across grass to follow a broad and obvious path into the trees again. At a wire fence the path bears right and later emerges via a barrier on to a suburban road. Keep ahead to a

T-junction, turn left along Elmbridge Drive and just after a right bend – and before a bridge – turn right through a fence gap  and walk along a path across meadows beside the little River Pinn. Pass through a line of trees, continue along the edge of the next stretch of meadowland and keep ahead to go through a metal gate on to a road .

Turn left here if returning to Ruislip Manor Station.

Turn right and then turn left by **Kings Café** and keep ahead across the grass keeping the metal fence on your left. Follow the path ahead where it bends left again, turn right and go through a hedge gap to continue alongside the river again. At the end of the meadow, go through a metal gate on to a road, cross over and take the straight, paved path ahead.

On reaching the end of a road ,

turn right along it (Sherwood Avenue) keep ahead at a crossroads, and at a T-junction pass through a barrier on to a path that re-enters Park Wood. Keep ahead and at a fork take the right-hand path and, ignoring all side paths, follow it to a crossway. Keep ahead here, and the path bears slightly left to reach a T-junction in front of Ruislip Lido. Originally constructed in 1811 as a feeder reservoir for the Grand Junction – later Grand Union – Canal, the lido is now a popular and attractive recreational amenity.

Turn left along a bridleway that keeps alongside a fence bordering the lido but look out for where you turn right through a fence gap to continue along a tarmac path across the end of the lido. Go through a gate on to a road and turn right to return to the start. ●

Ruislip Lido

Bexley and Joyden's Wood

		GPS waypoints
Start	Bexley Station	
Distance	5½ miles (8.2km)	TQ 493 734
Height gain	235 feet (70m)	Ⓐ TQ 484 727
		Ⓑ TQ 495 713
Approximate time	2½ hours	Ⓒ TQ 496 716
Parking	Pay and Display (free Sundays)	Ⓓ TQ 502 711
		Ⓔ TQ 501 718
Public transport	Trains from London (Charing Cross) to Bexley – South Eastern Trains	
Route terrain	Well defined paths through meadows and woodland	
Ordnance Survey maps	Landranger 177 (East London), Explorer 162 (Greenwich & Gravesend)	

This well-waymarked route follows a delightful stretch of the River Cray, where you may be lucky enough to glimpse a kingfisher, and then winds its way through ancient Joyden's Wood, which is ablaze with bluebells during springtime. There is also an opportunity to include a 1.2 mile circular Faesten Dic walk through the woodland.

With the station behind you turn right along Bexley High Street and almost immediately turn right, signposted Cray Riverway. Go under the railway bridge, pass to the right of Bexley Cricket Club and follow the path as it ascends an embankment, to a kissing-gate. Go through and the path later bears left down to another kissing-gate to reach a road Ⓐ.

Turn left between houses at a public footpath sign no.145 and follow an enclosed path. Cross a footbridge over the River Cray, go through a kissing-gate and turn right to go through another one. Keep ahead along a lovely stretch with the river on your right following the London Loop waymarks and at Five Arch Bridge turn left along a tarmac path and where the path forks bear left to a road (A223). Turn left, cross the road at the pedestrian lights and turn right along Parsonage Lane,

which continues left, uphill. Keep ahead for ½ mile and where the road veers left keep ahead along the rough track which joins a bridleway.

Ⓑ Turn left at a public footpath sign, no.137, go over the stile and bear left across the meadow to go over another stile. Cross a further stile and follow the path along the left edge of Joyden's Wood.

At a waymarked post turn right Ⓒ into the wood, go over a stile and take the narrow path ahead as it ascends and go over another stile. Cross the bridleway, go over the stile opposite and continue through woodland. At a crossing of paths turn right uphill. Go over a stile beside a metal gate and bear left along a bridleway looking out for waymarks on the right if you want to join the 1.2 mile circular walk through Faesten Dic. Otherwise, continue ahead and just before the bridleway curves right, turn left **D**, go over a stile beside a metal gate and at the next crossing of paths turn left, to a clearing where there is an information board about Faesten Dic.

This Scheduled Ancient Monument was constructed by Anglo Saxon settlers in Kent about 1,500 years ago to defend themselves against the Romano-British enemies who controlled London after the collapse of the Roman Empire. Originally the ditch was 26 feet wide and evidence suggests there was a gravel path so it's likely that it was patrolled.

Traces of Iron Age remains have also been discovered in Joyden's Wood.

Take the right-hand gravel path and at the next junction of paths turn right along a narrow downhill path, to a T-junction.

E Turn left and at the next T-junction turn right, pass beside a metal gate and continue to the right of Keepers Cottage. Go over a bar stile and at the bridleway turn right to pass between farm buildings to join a tarmac road. Cross the road (A2018) and rejoin the London Loop footpath opposite. Go through a kissing-gate and turn left to

Beside the River Cray in Joyden's Wood

Five Arch Bridge on the River Cray

go through another opposite the church of St Mary the Virgin.

Turn left and then right to continue

along Bexley High Street to return to the station car park. ●

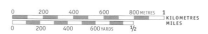

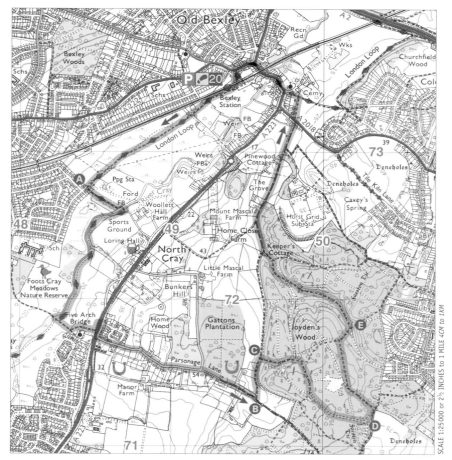

Epping Forest

Start	Queen Elizabeth's Hunting Lodge, on the A1069 to the east of Chingford
Distance	6 miles (9.7km). Add just over ½ mile (800m) if coming from Chingford Station
Height gain	360 feet (110m)
Approximate time	3 hours (3¼ hours from Chingford)
Parking	Car park opposite Queen Elizabeth's Hunting Lodge
Public transport	Trains from London (Liverpool Street) to Chingford. Turn right along the main road to the Queen Elizabeth Hunting Lodge car park
Route terrain	Sandy tracks and woodland paths
Ordnance Survey maps	Landranger 177 (East London), Explorer 174 (Epping Forest & Lee Valley)

GPS waypoints

- TQ 397 947
- Ⓐ TQ 401 951
- Ⓑ TQ 409 974
- Ⓒ TQ 411 982
- Ⓓ TQ 421 977
- Ⓔ TQ 419 970
- Ⓕ TQ 408 964

The grassland, glades and splendid woodlands of Epping Forest, once part of the vast royal hunting grounds of the Forest of Essex, are the setting for this walk. It takes you through an attractive and varied mixture of dense woodland and open grassland with some magnificent old trees and extensive views. As the forest is a public recreation area there are a multitude of paths and tracks but the absence of waymarking can cause confusion and make it difficult to stick to a precise route. For the most part this walk follows a clear and unambiguous route but there are places – especially in the vicinity of the Epping Forest Centre at High Beach – where the route directions need to be followed carefully.

During the Middle Ages the Forest of Essex, subsequently known as Waltham Forest, covered much of the county, and its proximity to the capital made it one of the most popular of royal hunting grounds. From the 17th century onwards, fellings and enclosures caused it to shrink rapidly and it became fragmented. The present Epping Forest is the largest of the remaining fragments, covering nearly 6,000 acres, and

was fortunately saved from further destruction by the Corporation of the City of London. By an Act of Parliament in 1878, the Corporation became the Conservators of Epping Forest in order to preserve it 'as an open space for the recreation and enjoyment of the public'. In the 18th century, Epping Forest was a favourite haunt of the notorious highwayman Dick Turpin.

Queen Elizabeth's Hunting Lodge, at

the start of the walk, was in fact built for Henry VIII as a grandstand from which to view the hunt.

👣 Begin by turning right out of the car park, cross the road and, just past a white building/former Butlers Retreat café, turn left on to a path that keeps to the left of a small pool and heads downhill across the open grassland of Chingford Plain. There are fine views ahead over the forest. The route is marked by white posts with horseshoes to indicate that this path is also available to riders. At a path junction  **A**, keep ahead. This is the Green Ride, and you follow this clear, broad, sandy track through the forest for the next 1½ miles, ignoring all side turns. The Green Ride keeps in a fairly straight line but look out for a fork, where you take the left-hand track. After following the track around right and left bends and keeping alongside an open area on the right, continue winding uphill through woodland to eventually emerge on to a road **B**.

Epping Forest

Turn left and, just before the road forks, turn right through a fence gap and walk along a path – waymarked with horseshoe posts – that keeps parallel to the road and is signposted to High Beach and Epping. At a T-junction, turn left to the road and turn right along it to the **King's Oak pub**. Across the open area to the left is a fine view, with the tower of Waltham Abbey clearly visible.

Just beyond the pub, turn right **C** along a tarmac drive to the Epping Forest Visitor Centre – plenty of books, maps and guides here – and at the entrance, turn left on to a specially constructed wheelchair path. Immediately bear right alongside a fence on the right – broken down and incomplete in places – bearing right at a fence corner. Turn left here along a path through an outstandingly beautiful area of woodland and, on reaching a track, turn left again. After about 200 yds turn right along a track that emerges on to the busy A104, opposite a parking area.

Cross the road and follow the path to the right of the parking area. Bear right on joining another path **D**, the Green Ride. After 200 yds turn right and then bear left through the woodland to reach the earthworks of Loughton Camp, an ancient fortification. Retrace your steps to the Green Ride and follow it gently uphill and past a track on the right **E**, to a road.

Cross over and continue along the track opposite, keeping to the left of a small pool. When you catch a glimpse of Strawberry Hill Pond on the right, turn right on to a path that keeps to the right of it to emerge into an open area. Bear left to follow the path across this open area into woodland again to a T-junction. Turn right on to a track and walk through a car park to the A104 again. Cross over, take the track opposite across another open area, cross a lane **F** and continue through woodland.

The track bears left. At a fork take the left-hand track, which later bears first left and then right and continues to a crossway. Turn left, here rejoining both the Green Ride and the outward route, and retrace your steps to the starting point. ●

Cassiobury Park and Whippendell Wood

		GPS waypoints
Start	Watford, by the railway bridge in Gade Avenue, just off the A412 between Watford and Rickmansworth	🖉 TQ 092 967 Ⓐ TQ 088 973 Ⓑ TQ 082 977
Distance	6 miles (9.7km). Add ½ mile (0.8km) if coming from Watford Station	Ⓒ TQ 069 978 Ⓓ TQ 066 981 Ⓔ TQ 067 970 Ⓕ TQ 088 964
Height gain	215 feet (65m)	
Approximate time	3 hours (3½ hours from Watford Station)	
Parking	Cassiobury Park car park	
Public transport	Underground to Watford (Metropolitan line). Turn left along Cassiobury Park Drive and bear right along Gade Avenue to reach the car park	
Route terrain	Woodland and riverside paths	
Ordnance Survey maps	Landranger 176 (West London), Explorer 172 (Chiltern Hills East)	

This highly attractive and enjoyable woodland, parkland and waterside walk is not far from the centre of Watford. At both the start and finish there are pleasant stretches along the banks of the River Gade and the Grand Union Canal, with some delightful areas of woodland in between. As a bonus, there is a pub almost exactly halfway round.

🖉 Begin by heading to the far left of the car park and turn right to join the tarmac path along the right bank of the River Gade and follow it through Cassiobury Park, keeping by the attractive, tree-lined riverbank. This fine area of parkland was once the estate of the earls of Essex but the great house was demolished in 1927.

Pass a footbridge and keep to the left of a children's play and picnic area to reach a crossing of paths just to the right of another footbridge.

Turn left to cross first the river and then the Grand Union Canal, keep ahead to a fork by a footpath post and take the right-hand path Ⓐ signposted public footpath 30. Keep along the main, tree-lined path all the while, initially just above the canal but then gradually bearing left away from it and heading gently uphill. After crossing several other paths, and part of the West Herts golf course, look out for where the path passes some picnic tables.

At a fork just beyond the picnic tables Ⓑ take the middle path, which descends through Whippendell Wood.

Whippendell Wood

Originally owned by the abbots of St Albans, this beautiful area of woodland passed to the earls of Essex following the dissolution of the monasteries in the 1530s. Like Cassiobury Park, it was later acquired for the people of Watford.

The multitude of paths through the wood can be confusing so it is important to take careful note of the following route directions. Keep ahead on the main path all the while until a fork where you take the right-hand path, passing through a glade and then into woodland again. Continue on the main path again – there are lots of side paths at this stage – and at a fork, just after the path starts to descend, keep along the wider right-hand path, which eventually emerges on to a lane **C**. Turn right along the narrow, tree-lined lane to a road and turn left into Chandler's Cross.

At a public footpath sign to Croxley Green, opposite **The Clarendon**, turn left through a kissing-gate **D** and walk along a narrow, enclosed path. Pass

through a fence gap to enter Harrocks Wood – owned by the Woodland Trust – and follow the path straight ahead

through another delightful area of woodland. Go through two kissing-gates on the far side, continue along an enclosed path that emerges on to a track in front of a house and continue along the track as far as a public footpath sign by a barn 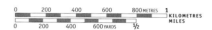.

Turn left through a kissing-gate, in the Rousebarn Lane direction, walk along an enclosed path. Keep ahead along a track through a belt of trees. The track then narrows to a path that continues along the right edge of a field. Keep straight ahead across the next field towards woodland and go through a kissing-gate on to a lane. Take the path opposite, which heads uphill through trees to emerge on the edge of the West Herts golf course again. The route continues in a straight line across the course, then through the next belt of trees, across another part of the course and finally down through more trees to the canal bridge 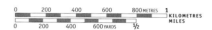.

From here you could simply retrace your steps to the start but for an attractive and more interesting option, turn left in front of the bridge down to the towpath and turn sharp right to pass under it, by Ironbridge Lock. Walk along the tranquil, tree-lined towpath as far as the next bridge (No. 168) and bear right in front of it up to a track 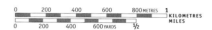.

Turn left to cross the bridge, continue along the track and at a fork take the left-hand path through woodland. Cross a footbridge over the River Gade and then turn left along a tarmac path to a crossway in front of another footbridge. Turn right to return to the car park or retrace your steps to the station. ●

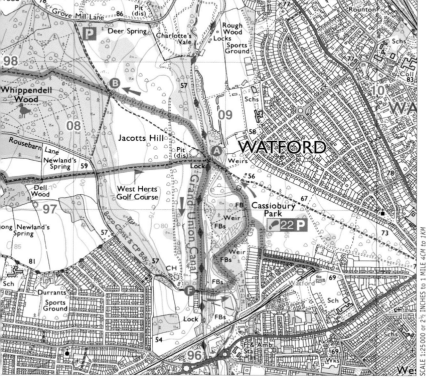

Farthing Downs and Happy Valley

Farthing Downs and Happy Valley

		GPS waypoints
Start	Farthing Downs, car park at the end of Downs Road 1¼ miles (2km) south of Coulsdon South Station	🏁 TQ 301 571
		Ⓐ TQ 302 571
Distance	6 miles (9.6km). Add 2½ miles (4km) if coming from Coulsdon South Station	Ⓑ TQ 311 564
		Ⓒ TQ 309 555
		Ⓓ TQ 305 550
		Ⓔ TQ 306 543
Height gain	460 feet (140m)	Ⓕ TQ 317 540
Approximate time	3 hours (4½ hours from Coulsdon South Station)	Ⓖ TQ 313 554
		Ⓗ TQ 314 563
Parking	Farthing Downs	Ⓙ TQ 303 572
Public transport	Trains from London (Victoria, Waterloo East and Charing Cross) to Coulsdon South. Turn right and, where the station forecourt curves left, bear right along a tarmac path. Descend steps to Marlpit Lane, turn right under a bridge, take the second road on the right (Downs Road) and head uphill on to Farthing Downs to the car park for the start	
Route terrain	Meadowland and woodland paths and tracks	
Ordnance Survey maps	Landranger 187 (Dorking & Reigate), Explorer 146 (Dorking, Box Hill & Reigate)	

This scenic and fairly energetic walk on the downs to the south of Croydon embraces a series of woodlands, the beautiful chalk meadowland of the secluded Happy Valley and grand views over the North Downs. It also passes the isolated medieval church at Chaldon and includes a stretch of the North Downs Way. The route is well-waymarked with 'Downlands Circular Walk' signs.

Farthing Downs, one of four commons near Coulsdon, is one of a number of areas of open country on the outskirts of the capital that are owned by the Corporation of the City of London. It has been maintained by the Corporation as a public recreation area since 1883.

🏁 From the car park cross the road and head down across the grass overlooked by a cottage and turn right on to a path Ⓐ at a public footpath sign to Devilsden Wood and Happy Valley. Pass beside a metal barrier to enter the sloping woodland.

At a fork, take the left-hand lower path, signposted to Happy Valley, continue through Devilsden Wood and,

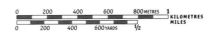

on emerging from it, keep ahead along the top right edge of the chalk grassland of Happy Valley. In the field corner – at a public footpath sign to Chaldon church – turn half-right into trees, bear left and continue along the right edge of grassland to the next field corner. Turn right Ⓑ, head uphill through a narrow belt of trees and continue more or less in a straight line across two fields. Re-enter woodland, head up to a lane, turn left and at a fork, take the right lane to pass to the left of Chaldon church.

This beautiful little flint church, which dates back to the 12th century, possesses one of the earliest known and best preserved wall paintings in England. The broach spire was not added until 1842.

Just after passing the church, turn left Ⓒ over a stile, at a public footpath sign to Alderstead Heath, and walk across a field to climb another stile. Bear slightly right across the next field and the path descends and bears left across to a stile. Climb it, keep in the same direction across the next field and, at a hedge corner, bear right along the right field edge and turn right through a kissing-gate into Furzefield Wood.

Keep ahead to cross a concrete track, and continue to pass between upright posts and at a crossway turn left in the Dean Lane direction. Where the track bears right, keep ahead along a path to climb a stile, and go half right to walk along the edge of a field – parallel to Dean Lane – and turn right through a kissing-gate on to the lane Ⓓ.

Cross over, take the concrete drive ahead to Tollsworth Manor Farm, and just past it turn left along a track into a field.

The track bears right at a house and continues along the right field edge. Go through a hedge gap, and ahead is a fine view over the North Downs. The built-up area on the opposite slopes is Redhill and Reigate. Turn left along the top field edge Ⓔ and continue along an enclosed, hedge-lined path, here joining the North Downs Way. Cross Hilltop Lane, take the track ahead, passing some large houses, and continue along an enclosed path into woodland. Keep along the right-hand path at a junction and look out for a public footpath sign to Rook Lane, where you leave the North Downs Way by turning left to a stile Ⓕ.

Climb the stile, walk along an enclosed path by woodland on the left and at a junction of five ways, keep ahead over a stile and continue along an enclosed path. After climbing the next stile, turn first right and then left, pass to the right of Rook Farm and climb another stile on to a road. Take the lane ahead (Doctors Lane) and after $\frac{1}{4}$ mile, turn right into Leazes Avenue Ⓖ. Continue along the left edge of a green at a fork and keep ahead along a track.

At a public bridleway sign to Happy Valley in front of gates, continue along a path through Piles Wood, heading gently downhill to emerge from the trees at the southern end of Happy Valley. At a footpath post, turn left Ⓗ through a hedge gap, in the Happy Valley direction, and walk along a springy, grassy path through the valley, a narrow belt of chalk grassland between gently sloping woodland. Keep ahead all the while and at a junction of paths by a stony track bear left Ⓙ and head steeply uphill through an area of grassland, trees and bushes.

At a crossway turn left, bear right and then bear left along a track, heading between blue-waymarked posts, up to Downs Road. Turn right here in order to retrace your steps back to the start. ●

Biggin Hill

		GPS waypoints
Start	Biggin Hill, Recreation Ground car park	📍 TQ 419 589
Distance	6½ miles (10.5km). Add ½ mile (800m) if coming by bus to Biggin Hill	Ⓐ TQ 432 591 Ⓑ TQ 431 577 Ⓒ TQ 444 569
Height gain	460 feet (140m)	Ⓓ TQ 451 567 Ⓔ TQ 443 577
Approximate time	3 hours (3¼ hours if coming by bus)	Ⓕ TQ 444 587 Ⓖ TQ 438 591
Parking	Recreation Ground car park off Church Road	
Public transport	Trains from London (Victoria) to Bromley South, bus to Biggin Hill (at time of printing no. 320) and walk along Church Road to the car park, which is on the left	
Route terrain	Good downland and woodland tracks and paths	
Ordnance Survey maps	Landranger 187 (Dorking & Reigate), Explorer 147 (Sevenoaks & Tonbridge)	

The walk explores the well-wooded and gently rolling country of the North Downs to the south and east of Biggin Hill. A short stretch of the North Downs Way is used, and from the crest of the downs the views across to the Kent Weald are superb, despite the unavoidable sight and sounds of the M25 in the valley below. This is a well-waymarked route, following regular 'Berry's Green Circular Walk' signs.

Biggin Hill has left an indelible mark on British history as one of the airfields that played a vital role in the Battle of Britain in 1940. The airport is just to the north of the village.

📍 Begin by turning left out of the car park along Church Road, turn left into Old Tye Avenue and immediately turn right along an enclosed path, at a public footpath sign to Berry's Green. Keep ahead – in a more or less straight line – across or along the edge of a succession of fields and over a series of stiles, finally climbing a stile in a field corner on to a track.

Continue along this track to a tarmac track and turn right Ⓐ in the South Street direction. Where the concrete track bears right to the Foal Animal Rescue Centre, keep ahead along a tree-lined path by the right edge of a golf course. At a crossing of paths, keep ahead across a field to the main road at South Street and turn left along it. At a public footpath sign to Knockholt, turn left along a drive Ⓑ and, in front of ornamental gates, bear right along an enclosed path.

Cross a track, keep ahead along another enclosed path, passing under a long green canopy, climb a stile, and another one immediately in front, and continue along an enclosed path to cross another stile. Cross a lane, climb the stile ahead, walk along the left edge of a field, by an interrupted hedge and line of trees on the left, and climb a stile in the field corner. Continue along an enclosed path, climb another stile and keep along the left edge of fields, climbing a series of stiles and heading down into a dip and up again. Finally walk across the middle of a field and climb a stile on to a lane.

Turn left and, at a public footpath sign, turn right **C** along a track to the left of a farmhouse. The track becomes enclosed, descends through trees and curves left to join the North Downs Way. After climbing a stile, keep ahead along the top edge of a steeply sloping field and from the crest of the downs there is a superb and extensive view to the right looking across the Kentish Weald. Climb a stile, continue through a belt of trees and keep along the left edge of a field. Follow the field edge to the right and, at a Berry's Green Circular Walk sign, turn left over a stile **D** – here leaving the North Downs Way – and continue across the next field to a stile.

Near Biggin Hill

Climb it, keep ahead, passing to the left of a house, to the corner of a lane and continue along it – there is a duck pond on the left – to a T-junction. Turn left and almost immediately turn right along Bombers Lane. Where the tarmac lane ends, turn left along a track – Old Harrow Lane – which narrows to become an enclosed path and continues through the attractive Shellem Wood, heading steadily downhill. At the bottom, turn right over a stile **E** at a

Berry's Green waymarker walk along the left edge of a field. Climb a stile, continue through an area of rough grassland, trees and bushes, climb another stile and bear left to keep along the top left edge of a field.

Continue – between trees on the left and a wire fence on the right – to a waymarked post and keep ahead to climb a stile on to a lane. Turn right and at a public footpath sign to Berry's Green **F** turn left up steps and over a stile and keep ahead across a field. Enter woodland, almost immediately climb a stile and follow a well-waymarked route through the wood to join an obvious path. Continue along it, turn left at a

three-way fork and keep along an undulating path to a lane. Turn right, follow the lane around left and right bends into Berry's Green and, at a public footpath sign 'Berry's Green Circular Walk, Short Walk', turn left over a stile **G**.

Bear slightly left across a field to climb a stile and keep ahead across the next field, making for a stile in the far left corner. Climb it and bear slightly right to follow a straight, waymarked route across a golf course, heading towards a footpath sign on the far side. After crossing two drives and climbing two stiles, pick up the outward route **A** and retrace your steps to the start. ●

Esher Common, Oxshott Heath and West End Common

		GPS waypoints
Start	West End Common, 1½ miles (2.4km) south of Esher on the A307	📝 TQ 125 626
		Ⓐ TQ 125 626
Distance	7 miles (11.3km). Add ½ mile (800m) if coming from Oxshott Station and pick up the walk at point Ⓒ	Ⓑ TQ 133 613
		Ⓒ TQ 138 609
		Ⓓ TQ 135 623
		Ⓔ TQ 121 625
Height gain	280 feet (85m)	Ⓕ TQ 121 629
Approximate time	3½ hours (3¾ hours from Oxshott Station)	Ⓖ TQ 128 639
		Ⓗ TQ 126 635
Parking	Horseshoe Clump car park on West End Common	
Public transport	Trains from London (Waterloo) to Oxshott. Turn right along the station drive, turn left into the Oxshott Heath Visitors Car Park and pass beside a barrier to follow a track into woodland. Bear left on meeting another track to emerge into open grassland and at a public footpath sign to Fairmile, bear right and then right again on to a more obvious path. Re-enter woodland, head gently uphill to a path junction and turn sharp right up steps to join the main route at point Ⓒ	
Route terrain	Good paths across common land	
Ordnance Survey maps	Landranger 176 (West London), Explorer 161 (London South)	

The three adjacent commons of Esher, West End and Oxshott Heath, collectively known as Elmbridge Commons, are remnants of the extensive heathlands that used to cover much of western Surrey. In the past such areas were regarded with horror by travellers but now they are seen as rare examples of a rural wilderness that needs to be zealously preserved. This figure-of-eight walk can easily be split into two separate shorter walks but the proliferation of paths and tracks across the commons requires you to follow the route directions carefully.

📝 Facing the road, start by taking the path that leads off from the bottom right-hand corner of the car park, passing beside a barrier. At a crossing of paths, turn left down to the road Ⓐ cross it, pass between a barrier, at a public footpath sign to Oxshott Heath, and take a path through the woodlands of Esher Common, bearing right at a fork to follow a yellow-waymarked route.

Keep ahead at the first crossway and at the second one pass beside a barrier and continue along the right edge of Black Pond, which is a haven for wildlife. Pass beside another barrier on to a broad track, bear left, in the Oxshott Heath direction, and the track becomes tarmacked, ascending and

turning right to cross a bridge over the busy A3. Continue ahead to re-enter woodland and, at a fork by the next sign, take the right-hand path. Continue along an enclosed path between fences, pass beside a barrier on to a road, turn left, cross the road and almost immediately turn right **B** along another enclosed path. The path emerges briefly adjacent a road, bears

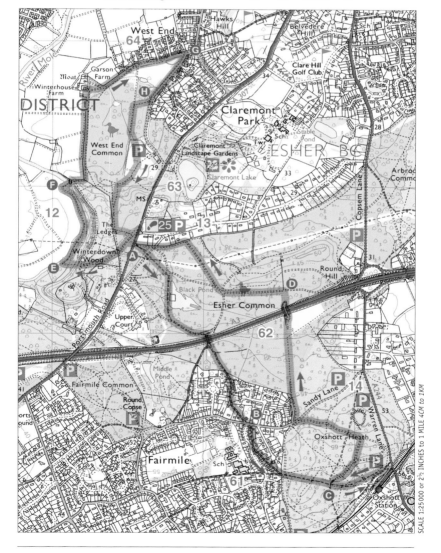

left and continues to the edge of Oxshott Heath. Bear left to a junction. Here a blue-waymarked post indicates a 'Horse Ride' on the right but the route keeps straight ahead across the heath, heading first uphill and then descending to a crossway **C**.

If returning to Oxshott Station, keep ahead to retrace your earlier route.

At the crossway, turn left to ascend steps and keep ahead along a ridge. From here there are grand views to the right across the heath. At a junction of paths by a war memorial, bear left on to a path that passes to the right of it – there is a white-waymarked Trail 2000 post here – and at a crossway by another Trail 2000 post, turn sharp left, looking out for a Horse Ride sign on a tree trunk ahead. Follow the bridleway and descend to a junction and another waymarked post. Keep ahead along a path – there is another Horse Ride sign attached to a tree – which bears left to a road and at a Horse Ride post turn right to cross the road.

Take the path opposite, signposted to Esher Common, which soon broadens out into a wide sandy track, and follow it in a straight line across the heath. It becomes a tarmac track that crosses the A3 and then reverts to a sandy track. After 50 yds at a crossway turn left **D**, continue to a junction (Five Ways) and turn half-right, in the direction of Black Pond. Keep ahead and at a T-junction, turn left to continue along the right edge of the common. At a crossway, turn right to pick up the outward route and keep ahead through a barrier to the A307 **A**.

Cross over and continue through the trees of West End Common to a crossway. Horseshoe Clump car park is just to the right but the route continues to the left along a fairly straight and wide path to a T-junction. Turn left,

take the first path on the right, pass through a barrier and descend steps to the banks of the River Mole **E**. Turn right alongside the river – there are boardwalks in places – and look out for a fork where you turn right away from it **F** and ascend steps to pass beside another barrier. From here there are fine views over the Mole valley.

Pass a footpath post, bear slightly right along the left, inside edge of the common, and the path curves left to a T-junction. Turn left to keep along the left edge of the woodland to a barrier and beyond that continue along a tarmac drive. Pass under a metal barrier to the right of Winterhouse Farm, turn right at a T-junction and continue along a tarmac drive to emerge from the trees on to the edge of the large green at West End. This picturesque spot has all the ingredients that make up a traditional English village green: pub, duck pond, cricket pitch and church. The latter is a small, white-painted corrugated iron structure built in 1879.

Walk along the left edge of the green, turn right **G** at the **Prince of Wales pub**, keep past the church and, after passing a pond on the right, turn right **H**, and head into woodland again. At a crossway, turn left along a straight path, with ditches both sides, turn left to cross a ditch, go up steps, pass through a fence gap and bear right to continue across rough grassland. The path curves left to a T-junction, where you turn right on to a clearer path, re-entering woodland.

Bear right to another T-junction in front of a mound, turn left along a path that bears right steeply uphill and keep ahead at the top. Bear left on joining another path and at a fork take the left-hand path to emerge into a clearing. Turn left on to a path that heads downhill to the start. ●

Colne Valley, South Harefield and Bayhurst Wood

		GPS waypoints
Start	Denham Country Park, Colne Valley Visitor Centre	🖉 TQ 047 864
Distance	7 miles (11.3km). Add 1½ miles (2.4km) if coming from Denham Station and pick up the walk at the bridge over the Grand Union Canal at South Harefield near point Ⓑ	Ⓐ TQ 053 866 Ⓑ TQ 051 887 Ⓒ TQ 052 897 Ⓓ TQ 068 892 Ⓔ TQ 068 880
Height gain	360 feet (110m)	Ⓕ TQ 071 871 Ⓖ TQ 063 870
Approximate time	3½ hours (4½ hours from Denham Station)	
Parking	Denham Country Park	
Public transport	Trains from London (Marylebone) to Denham. From the station platform, turn left under the tunnel, descend more steps and walk along a tarmac path to a lane. Turn left to a T-junction, turn right and follow the road to the canal bridge to join the main route near point Ⓑ	
Route terrain	Towpath, woodland paths prone to mud	
Dog friendly	Care needed as cattle are present in some fields	
Ordnance Survey maps	Landranger 176 (West London), Explorer 172 (Chiltern Hills East)	

From the pleasant environs of Denham Country Park, the route first follows the towpath of the Grand Union Canal to South Harefield. It then heads across to Bayhurst Wood, a remnant of the ancient Forest of Middlesex, and on the final leg you pass some pools created from gravel extraction, now an attractive feature of the Colne Valley. The fine open views and rural nature of this walk convey something of the flavour of John Betjeman's largely vanished 'Rural Middlesex'. There may be mud in places.

Denham Country Park is part of the Colne Valley Regional Park. The latter, stretching along the western outskirts of London, was established in 1965 to make the Colne Valley a greener and more attractive area and to improve its facilities for outdoor activities.

🖉 The walk begins in front of the visitor centre. With your back to it head towards the road. Cross a road to the left of a bridge and go through the gate opposite. The path turns left away from the river to a crossing of paths.

Keep ahead along the bridleway, which runs along the right edge of woodland, curving right, and at a path junction and Grand Union Canal waymark turn left on to a track into the trees. The track bends right to cross a footbridge over the River Colne and continues winding through this attractive woodland. Shortly after a right bend, you reach a footpath sign to Denham Quarry. Turn right to the towpath of the Grand Union Canal and turn left on to it **Ⓐ**, passing under bridge 182. Follow the towpath for 1¼ miles, going under a railway bridge and passing Harefield Marina. In front of the first road bridge, bear left and climb steps to the road, where the walk briefly follows the London Loop path.

If returning to Denham Station, turn left here and retrace your outward route.

Turn right over the bridge by Widewater Lock and, after passing to the right of modern factory buildings, turn left on to a concrete path **Ⓑ** that runs along the left edge of a recreation ground. The path later becomes enclosed between wire fences and emerges on to a road. Turn right and at a T-junction cross the main road, pass beside a metal gate, at a public footpath sign, and take the gently ascending track ahead. In front of a metal gate, follow the track to the left, passing the Australian Military Cemetery on the right. Many Australian soldiers wounded in the Gallipoli landings in 1915 were sent to Harefield for hospital treatment and died from their wounds. The track emerges on to a tarmac drive by an attractive brick and flint church of medieval origin.

Walk along the drive as far as a Hillingdon Trail sign, turn right **Ⓒ** and keep ahead along an enclosed path, by the wall of the churchyard on the right, and continue through woodland, passing to the right of some stagnant pools and through a kissing-gate. Continue through trees and, after emerging from them at a Hillingdon Trail sign, bear right and keep along the left edge of a field, then bear right in the

field corner to continue along the left field edge – later by trees – to a stile at the corner of the woodland. Climb it, immediately turn left over another stile and keep ahead along the right edge of woodland, heading downhill to a stile in the bottom corner of the field.

Climb the stile, turn left and then immediately right and follow a path through the trees to climb another stile. Turn left to continue along the right edge of woodland, and the path passes beside two fences to enter Bayhurst Wood Country Park. Keep ahead near the left, inside edge of the wood, following Hillingdon Trail signs. After passing an information board, turn right **Ⓓ** at the next Hillingdon Trail sign on to a wide path that continues through this beautiful area of woodland. Keep ahead on the main path all the while, descending to a crossing of paths and tracks on the far side of the wood and in front of a pond.

Do not turn left on to the track – there is a Hillingdon Trail sign here – but cross the track to the pond and then turn left on to a path that keeps along the right inside edge of the trees. Pass a picnic and barbecue area, continue via a kissing-gate to a T-junction and turn right along a winding track – this may be muddy in places – which emerges on to a lane. Turn right and, where the lane bends to the right, bear left **Ⓔ** on to a track, at a public bridleway sign. This tree-lined track first ascends and then descends to reach a concrete drive. Keep ahead to a busy road, turn right to pass under a railway bridge and, at a public footpath sign about 100 yds beyond, turn right along a tarmac drive to a stile **Ⓕ**.

Climb the stile and continue along the drive, which turns left. Where the drive ends, climb the stile ahead – by a pond – and walk along the left edge of a

field. The path, which later becomes enclosed, continues to a stile. Climb it, keep ahead through a belt of trees to climb another one and bear right along the right edge of the next field, by a hedge on the right. Go through a kissing-gate, head across a field, climb another stile on the far side and continue across the next field to climb a stile on to a road **G**.

Climb the stile opposite, continue across a field and climb two more stiles to reach the edge of a golf-course. Keep ahead to join a track and follow it gently downhill across the course.

Continue through a belt of trees and, at a public footpath sign, turn right and walk across the grass, making for some trees. Follow a track through an area of trees and bushes, cross a causeway between two pools, continue over a track and cross a footbridge over a stream.

Walk across another causeway and, on the far side, keep ahead to the canal. Cross the canal bridge **A** to rejoin the outward route back to the start. ●

Richmond Park

		GPS waypoints
Start	Richmond Station	TQ 180 751
Distance	8 miles (13km)	Ⓐ TQ 177 745
Height gain	425 feet (130m)	Ⓑ TQ 181 733
Approximate time	4 hours	Ⓒ TQ 187 727
Parking	NCP car park next to the station	Ⓓ TQ 191 718
Public transport	Underground (District line) or rail (from Waterloo) to Richmond Station	Ⓔ TQ 198 711
		Ⓕ TQ 211 722
Route terrain	Thames Path, heathland paths, pavements	Ⓖ TQ 185 736
Dog friendly	Caution needed in the vicinity of deer especially during the rutting season, September – November	
Ordnance Survey maps	Landranger 176 (West London), Explorer 161 (London South)	

The route follows the river for a short while then veers across Petersham Meadows before continuing along unfenced roadside paths and a section of the Capital Ring footpath. The varied landscape includes ponds, heathland, plantations and the remarkable view from the Mound.

With your back to the station turn left along the main road. Go over the pedestrian crossing turning right then immediately left through Old Station Passage, turning left again into

Richmond Green

Parkshot. Follow the sign for the river keeping to the left-hand side of Richmond Green and on into Friars Lane, following its twisting course down to the Thames. Turn left and head on to pass under Richmond Bridge Ⓐ and with the river on your right, follow the Thames Path as it veers left. At a signpost to Petersham go through a kissing-gate and follow the tarmac path across the meadow to another kissing-gate. Go through and keep ahead along an enclosed path, pass a church, and at the road turn left Ⓑ.

At the **Dysart Arms**

The view west from the Henry VIII Mound

pub cross the road and enter Richmond Park on the right through a metal gate.

At almost 2,500 acres Richmond Park is the largest of the royal parks and home to more than 600 deer. Charles I introduced red and fallow deer in the 17th century when he came here from London to escape the plague and although he enclosed the land, he did allow pedestrians the right of way.

Bear half left uphill along a grass path and at the top go through a metal gate into Pembroke Lodge Gardens. To see the remarkable view across to St Paul's Cathedral dome from Henry VIII's Mound, turn left and at a T-junction turn left again, then first right towards a white signpost that points towards the Mound. From here is a protected view of the dome of St Paul's Cathedral, 10 miles away. King Henry VIII was said to have stood here when his wife, Anne Boleyn, was beheaded at the Tower of London.

To continue the walk retrace your steps to the gate and with this on your right continue through the gardens and go through a gate at the far end ⒸＣ.

Keep ahead along a gravel track flanked by ancient oak trees. The path descends to the right of a road and at Ham Cross turn left in the direction of Isabella Plantation. Take the first path on the right ⒹＤ, and walk gently uphill beside a wide bridleway with horse chestnut trees to your left and heathland to your right. At a crossing of paths keep ahead, pass a wire fence on the right surrounding a small pond, and continue uphill to a tarmac road ⒺＥ.

Here turn left along a path beside the road and later pass to the left of a car park. Keep ahead as the road descends and there are good views of Central London from here. The path later curves first right and then left to reach a mini roundabout ⒻＦ.

Turn first left and continue on a path beside the tarmac road. Pass to the right of a small pool and after the car park turn left along a gently descending gravel path towards Pen Ponds.

Cross the causeway between the ponds and then head uphill. At the top take the path that runs beside a road on the right. Follow the road to a roundabout and turn right to leave Richmond Park

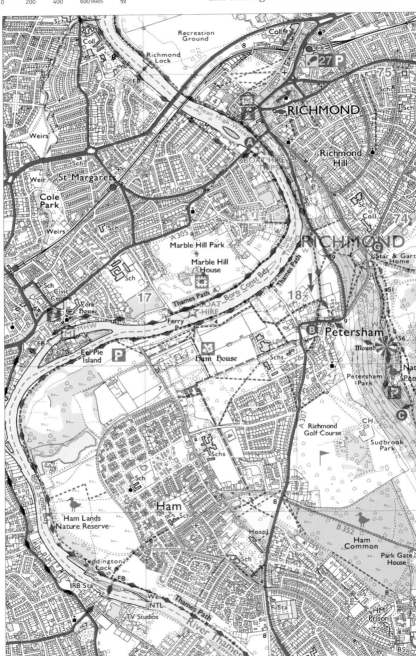

through Richmond Gate **G**.

Cross the road and keep ahead down Richmond Hill past Terrace Field on the left where there is a good viewpoint, and then descend steps to enter Terrace Gardens. These are famous for their seasonal shrubberies and rose garden and at the top of the terrace is a modern statue of Aphrodite, nicknamed 'Bulbous Betty'. On a clear day, with the aid of the telescope here, you can see Windsor Castle.

Continue ahead and at Cardigan Gate

Bulbous Betty in the Terrace Garden

turn right on to the pavement and continue down Richmond Hill where you can follow the main road back to Richmond Station.

Cudham and Downe

		GPS waypoints	
Start	High Elms Country Park	✏	TQ 446 634
Distance	8 miles (12.9km)	Ⓐ	TQ 443 629
Height gain	755 feet (230m)	Ⓑ	TQ 454 611
Approximate time	4 hours	Ⓒ	TQ 445 597
Parking	At start	Ⓓ	TQ 435 599
		Ⓔ	TQ 429 612
Public transport	Trains from London (Victoria) to	Ⓕ	TQ 430 621
	Bromley South, bus 146 to Downe	Ⓖ	TQ 432 630
	and pick up the walk by the church	Ⓗ	TQ 438 631
	in Downe village		
Route terrain	Woodland tracks and field paths; some steep ascents and descents		
Ordnance Survey maps	Landrangers 177 (East London) and 178 (Thames Estuary), Explorer 147 (Sevenoaks & Tonbridge)		

From High Elms Country Park the route proceeds through woodland and across fields to Cudham. It continues to Downe, passing Charles Darwin's house, and returns to the start by way of tracks and field paths. Both villages have fine medieval churches, and there are splendid views extending from the Thames basin to the North Downs. It is quite an energetic walk but well waymarked as most of it follows the frequent 'Cudham Circular Walk' signs.

High Elms Country Park is based on the former estate of the Lubbock family. Sir John William Lubbock built the house and laid out the grounds in the Italian style in the 1840s. In 1938 the estate passed into local authority ownership and, although the house was burned down in 1967, the formal gardens and stables remain.

✏ At the far end of the car park, turn right beside a barrier on to a tarmac track and, at a crossway and London Loop post, turn right to follow a curving track uphill through the ornamental gardens. Where the tarmac track ends, turn right across the grass and continue between hedges to a kissing-gate. Go through, walk through the car park of the High Elms Golf Club to a lane and turn left.

Just after passing the unusual High Elms Clockhouse, turn left on to a track Ⓐ at a public bridleway sign to Cudham Lane North and continue along an enclosed, fence-lined path across the golf course to enter Cuckoo Wood. Turn right beside a barrier to continue through this beautiful woodland (awash with bluebells in spring), turn left at a crossway by a footpath sign, turn left again at a T-junction and head downhill. Where the path curves left, turn right, at a yellow waymark, to continue downhill, keep ahead at a crossway and continue to a barrier. Pass under it, keeping ahead uphill along the right edge of a field. In the field corner turn right through a metal kissing-gate on to a lane.

Turn right and then immediately left along Snag Lane. Where the lane turns right, keep ahead along an enclosed path, at a public bridleway sign to Knockholt and Pratt's Bottom. Descend under a canopy of trees and follow a curving and undulating path to a

SCALE 1:26316 or 2½ INCHES to 1 MILE 3.8CM to 1KM

T-junction **B**. Turn right through a belt of trees and continue along the right edge of a field – later the path becomes a concrete one. After passing to the left

Looking downhill towards Single Street

of cottages and a farm, keep ahead along a lane that curves right. At a public footpath sign to Cudham church, turn left.

As you continue along an enclosed path, there are distant views to the right of the Thames basin, with the tower blocks of the East End and the tower of Canary Wharf clearly visible. The path continues diagonally across a field to a kissing-gate. Go through, head across the next field and on the far side go through another metal kissing-gate. Cross a tarmac drive, go through another metal kissing-gate and turn right along the right edge of a playing field. There is a fine view of Cudham church ahead as you follow the edge of the playing field to the left to a public footpath sign. This delightful flint church, small but quite wide, dates back to the 12th century and is unusual in that the central tower is on the south side.

Continue along a tarmac path by the field edge, pass beside a barrier into a car park and turn right to a lane **C**. Turn right and, opposite the **Blacksmiths Arms**, turn left at a public footpath sign to Biggin Hill, go over a stile and bear right downhill across a field to climb another stile. Continue steeply downhill through trees, climb a stile and turn left along a lane. Head down into a dip, then continue gently uphill and at a public footpath sign to Luxted and Downe, bear right through a squeezer-stile and head steeply uphill along a tree-lined tarmac drive. At a yellow waymark, turn right up steps, climb a stile and continue along an enclosed path that turns left and continues uphill. Bear right along a track to a road and turn right through Single Street.

At a public footpath sign by a right bend, turn left **D** in the Biggin Hill direction, along a narrow, enclosed path, follow it around left- and right-hand bends and continue to a stile. Climb it, turn right, go over another stile and then along the right edge of a field, climb another stile and continue along an enclosed path to a stile. Climb another stile, keep ahead along a track to a lane, turn left and, where the lane bends right, keep ahead downhill along a tree-lined tarmac track.

Turn right, at a public footpath sign to Downe along a hedge-and tree-lined path. The path continues first along the left edge of a field, then through woodland, then along the right edge of a golf course and re-enters trees to reach a crossway. Turn right, in the Downe direction, and head uphill – via steps – to a stile. Climb it and continue uphill, curving left and crossing a field to climb another stile.

For walkers who wish to visit Down House, turn right through a gate, turn left through another gate and walk through the grounds to the house. This was for 40 years the home of Charles Darwin, and here is the study in which he wrote *On the Origin of Species by Natural Selection* in 1859.

After climbing the stile, the route continues along an enclosed path to a lane. Turn right along it to a road and turn left **E** into the village of Downe, which has some attractive flint cottages, two pubs and a 13th-century church. *Those coming by bus join and leave the walk at this point.* The road curves left in the village centre and about $\frac{1}{2}$ mile

farther on – where the road bears left – turn right **F**, at a public footpath sign to Farnborough, on to a tree-lined and enclosed path that bears left and continues to a waymarked post. Pass beside it to walk along the left edge of a field and, at the next post, turn left through a wide hedge gap and continue across the next field to a kissing-gate.

Go through it, cross a track, take the enclosed path opposite and, at a junction of paths, turn sharp right up steps **G** – here rejoining the London Loop – and turn left along the left edge of a field. Descend steps in the field corner, turning left down to an enclosed track, and turn right along it to a lane. Turn left and, at a public footpath sign to High Elms, turn right **H** along an enclosed, uphill, tree-lined path.

Continue, keep ahead through another belt of delightful woodland and the path descends across part of the High Elms golf course again to a lane opposite the Clockhouse **A**. Turn left and retrace your steps through the Country Park to the start.   ●

Woodland near High Elms

Further Information

The National Trust

Anyone who likes visiting places of natural beauty and/or historic interest has cause to be grateful to the National Trust. Without it, many such places would probably have vanished by now.

It was in response to the pressures on the countryside posed by the relentless march of Victorian industrialisation that the trust was set up in 1895. Its founders, inspired by the common goals of protecting and conserving Britain's national heritage and widening public access to it, were Sir Robert Hunter, Octavia Hill and Canon Rawnsley: respectively a solicitor, a social reformer and a clergyman. The latter was particularly influential. As a canon of Carlisle Cathedral and vicar of Crosthwaite (near Keswick), he was concerned about threats to the Lake District and had already been active in protecting footpaths and promoting public access to open countryside. After the flooding of Thirlmere in 1879 to create a large reservoir, he became increasingly convinced that the only effective way to guarantee protection was outright ownership of land.

The purpose of the National Trust is to preserve areas of natural beauty and sites of historic interest by acquisition, holding them in trust for the nation and making them available for public access and enjoyment. Some of its properties have been acquired through purchase, but many have come to the Trust as donations. Nowadays, it is not only one of the biggest landowners in the country, but also one of the most active conservation charities, protecting 581,113 acres (253,176 ha) of land, including 555 miles (892km) of coastline, and over 300 historic properties in England, Wales and Northern Ireland. (There is a separate National Trust for Scotland, which was set up in 1931.)

Furthermore, once a piece of land has come under National Trust ownership, it is difficult for its status to be altered. As a result of parliamentary legislation in 1907, the Trust was given the right to declare its property inalienable, so ensuring that in any subsequent dispute it can appeal directly to parliament.

As it works towards its dual aims of conserving areas of attractive countryside and encouraging greater public access (not easy to reconcile in this age of mass tourism), the Trust provides an excellent service for walkers by creating new concessionary paths and waymarked trails, maintaining stiles and footbridges and combating the ever-increasing problem of footpath erosion.

For details of membership, contact the National Trust at the address on page 94.

The Ramblers

No organisation works more actively to protect and extend the rights and interests of walkers in the countryside than the Ramblers. Its aims are clear: to foster a greater knowledge, love and care of the countryside; to assist in the protection and enhancement of public rights of way and areas of natural beauty; to work for greater public access to the countryside; and to encourage more people to take up rambling as a healthy, recreational leisure activity.

It was founded in 1935 when, following the setting up of a National Council of Ramblers' Federations in 1931, a number of federations earlier formed in London, Manchester, the Midlands and elsewhere came together to create a more effective pressure group, to deal with such problems as the disappearance and obstruction of footpaths, the prevention of access to open mountain and moorland and increasing hostility from landowners. This was the era of the mass trespasses, when there were sometimes violent confrontations between ramblers and gamekeepers, especially on the moorlands of the Peak District.

Since then the Ramblers has played an influential role in preserving and developing the national footpath network, supporting the creation of national parks and encouraging the designation and waymarking of long-distance routes.

Our freedom to walk in the countryside is precarious and requires constant vigilance. As well as the perennial problems of footpaths being illegally obstructed, disappearing through lack of use or extinguished by housing or road construction, new dangers can spring up at any time.

It is to meet such problems and dangers that the Ramblers exists and represents the interests of all walkers. The address to write to for information on the Ramblers and how to become a member is given on page 94.

Walkers and the Law

The Countryside and Rights of Way Act (CRoW Act 2000) extends the rights of access previously enjoyed by walkers in England and Wales. Implementation of these rights began on 19 September 2004. The Act amends existing legislation and for the first time provides access on foot to certain types of land – defined as mountain, moor, heath, down and registered common land.

Where You Can Go
Rights of Way
Prior to the introduction of the CRoW Act, walkers could only legally access the countryside along public rights of way. These are either 'footpaths' (for walkers only) or 'bridleways' (for walkers, riders on horseback and pedal cyclists). A third category called 'Byways open to all traffic' (BOATs), is used by motorised vehicles as well as those using non-mechanised transport. Mainly they are green lanes, farm and estate roads, although occasionally they will be found crossing mountainous area.

Rights of way are marked on Ordnance Survey maps. Look for the green broken lines on the Explorer maps, or the red dashed lines on Landranger maps.

The term 'right of way' means exactly what it says. It gives a right of passage over what, for the most part, is private land. Under pre-CRoW legislation walkers were required to keep to the line of the right of way and not stray onto land on either side. If you did inadvertently wander off the right of way, either because of faulty map reading or because the route was not clearly indicated on the ground, you were technically trespassing.

Local authorities have a legal obligation to ensure that rights of way are kept clear and free of obstruction, and are signposted where they leave metalled roads. The duty of local authorities to install signposts extends to the placing of signs along a path or way, but only where the authority considers it necessary to have a signpost or waymark to assist persons unfamiliar with the locality.

The New Access Rights
Access Land
As well as being able to walk on existing rights of way, under the new legislation you now have access to large areas of open land. You can of course continue to use rights of way footpaths to cross this land, but the main difference is that you can now lawfully leave the path and wander at will, but only in areas designated as access land.

Where to Walk
Areas now covered by the new access rights – Access Land – are shown on Ordnance Survey Explorer maps bearing 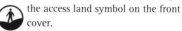 the access land symbol on the front cover.

'Access Land' is shown on Ordnance Survey maps by a light yellow tint surrounded by a pale orange border. New orange coloured 'i' symbols on the maps will show the location of permanent access information boards installed by the access authorities.

Restrictions
The right to walk on access land may lawfully be restricted by landowners. Landowners can, for any reason, restrict access

for up to 28 days in any year.
They cannot however close the land:

- on bank holidays;
- for more than four Saturdays and Sundays in a year;
- on any Saturday from 1 June to 11 August; or
- on any Sunday from 1 June to the end of September.

They have to provide local authorities with five working days' notice before the date of closure unless the land involved is an area of less than five hectares or the closure is for less than four hours. In these cases landowners only need to provide two hours' notice.

Whatever restrictions are put into place on access land they have no effect on existing rights of way, and you can continue to walk on them.

Dogs

Dogs can be taken on access land, but must be kept on leads of two metres or less between 1 March and 31 July, and at all times where they are near livestock. In addition landowners may impose a ban on all dogs from fields where lambing takes place for up to six weeks in any year. Dogs may be banned from moorland used for grouse shooting and breeding for up to five years.

In the main, walkers following the routes in this book will continue to follow existing rights of way, but a knowledge and understanding of the law as it affects

---

 ## Countryside Access Charter

Your rights of way are:

- public footpaths – on foot only. Sometimes waymarked in yellow
- bridle-ways – on foot, horseback and pedal cycle. Sometimes waymarked in blue
- byways (usually old roads), most 'roads used as public paths' and, of course, public roads – all traffic has the right of way

Use maps, signs and waymarks to check rights of way. Ordnance Survey Explorer and Landranger maps show most public rights of way

On rights of way you can:

- take a pram, pushchair or wheelchair if practicable
- take a dog (on a lead or under close control)
- take a short route round an illegal obstruction or remove it sufficiently to get past

You have a right to go for recreation to:

- public parks and open spaces – on foot
- most commons near older towns and cities – on foot and sometimes on horseback
- private land where the owner has a formal agreement with the local authority

In addition you can use the following by local or established custom or consent, but ask for advice if you are unsure:

- many areas of open country, such as moorland, fell and coastal areas, especially those in the care of the National Trust, and some commons
- some woods and forests, especially those owned by the Forestry Commission
- country parks and picnic sites
- most beaches
- canal towpaths
- some private paths and tracks Consent sometimes extends to horse-riding and cycling

For your information:

- county councils and London boroughs maintain and record rights of way, and register commons
- obstructions, dangerous animals, harassment and misleading signs on rights of way are illegal and you should report them to the county council
- paths across fields can be ploughed, but must normally be reinstated within two weeks
- landowners can require you to leave land to which you have no right of access
- motor vehicles are normally permitted only on roads, byways and some 'roads used as public paths'

A heron at Richmond slipway

walkers, plus the ability to distinguish access land marked on the maps, will enable anyone who wishes to depart from paths that cross access land either to take a shortcut, to enjoy a view or to explore.

General Obstructions

Obstructions can sometimes cause a problem on a walk and the most common of these is where the path across a field has been ploughed over. It is legal for a farmer to plough up a path provided that it is restored within two weeks. This does not always happen and you are faced with the dilemma of following the line of the path, even if this means treading on crops, or walking round the edge of the field. Although the latter course of action seems the most sensible, it does mean that you would be trespassing.

Other obstructions can vary from overhanging vegetation to wire fences across the path, locked gates or even a cattle feeder on the path.

Use common sense. If you can get round the obstruction without causing damage, do so. Otherwise only remove as much of the obstruction as is necessary to secure passage.

If the right of way is blocked and cannot be followed, there is a long-standing view that in such circumstances there is a right to deviate, but this cannot wholly be relied on. Although it is accepted in law that highways (and that includes rights of way) are for the public service, and if the usual track is impassable, it is for the general good that people should be entitled to pass into another line. However, this should not be taken as indicating a right to deviate whenever a way becomes impassable. If in doubt, retreat.

Report obstructions to the local authority and/or the Ramblers.

 ### Walking Safety

Although the reasonably gentle countryside that is the subject of this book offers no real dangers to walkers at any time of the year, it is still advisable to take sensible precautions and follow certain well-tried guidelines.

Always take with you both warm and waterproof clothing and sufficient food and drink. Wear suitable footwear, such as strong walking boots or shoes that give a good grip over stony ground, on slippery slopes and in muddy conditions. Try to obtain a local weather forecast and bear it in mind before you start. Do not be afraid to abandon your proposed route and return to your starting point in the event of unexpected bad weather.

All the walks described in this book will be safe to do, given due care and respect, even during the winter. Indeed, a crisp, fine winter day often provides perfect walking conditions, with firm ground underfoot and a clarity that is not possible to achieve at any other time of the year.

The most difficult hazard likely to be encountered is mud, especially when walking along woodland and field paths, farm tracks and bridleways – the latter in particular can often get churned up by cyclists and horses. In summer, an additional difficulty may be narrow and overgrown paths, particularly along the edges of cultivated fields. Neither should constitute a major problem provided that the appropriate footwear is worn.

 Useful Organisations

Visit Britain HQ
Thames Tower, Black's Road,
Hammersmith, London W9 6EL
Tel. 0208 846 9000
www.visitbritain.com

Campaign to Protect Rural England
128 Southwark Street, London SE1 0SW
Tel. 0207 981 2800
www.cpre.org.uk

English Heritage
1 Waterhouse Square, 138-142 Holborn,
London EC1N 2ST
Tel. 020 7973 3000
www.english-heritage.org.uk

Forestry Commission
Silvan House, 231 Corstorphine Road,
Edinburgh EH14 5NE
Tel. 0845 367 3787
www.forestry.gov.uk

**London Tourist Board &
Convention Bureau**
26 Grosvenor Gardens, Victoria SW1
Tel. 0207 932 2000
www.londonby.com

VisitLondon
2 More London Riverside, London
Tel. 020 723 458 000
www.visitlondon.com

Tourist information centres:
Bexley: 01322 558676
Croydon: 0208 253 1009
Greenwich: 0870 608 2000
Harrow: 0208 424 1102
Hillingdon: 01895 250706
Hounslow: 0845 4562929
Kingston Upon Thames: 0208 547 5592
Lewisham: 0208 297 8317
Richmond: 0208 940 9125
Twickenham: 0208 891 7272

Long Distance Walkers' Association
www.ldwa.org.uk

National Trust
Membership and general enquiries:
PO Box 39, Warrington WA5 7WD
Tel. 0870 458 4000
www.nationaltrust.org.uk
Thames and Chilterns Regional Office:
Hughenden Manor, High Wycombe,
Bucks HP14 4LA
Tel. 01494 528051

Ordnance Survey
Romsey Road, Maybush, Southampton
SO16 4GU
Tel. 08456 05 05 05 (Lo-call)
www.ordnancesurvey.co.uk

Ramblers
2nd Floor, Camelford House,
87–90 Albert Embankment, London
SE1 7TW
Tel. 0207 339 8500
www.ramblers .org.uk

Transport for London
Comprehensive journey planning information throughout London by Underground, rail, bus, DLR, tram and river is available on the Transport for London website www.tfl.gov.uk

Underground maps can be printed from the website for personal use.

London Travel Information
Tel. 0843 222 1234
Email: travinfo@tfl.gov.uk

Visit London
2 More London Riverside, London
Tel. 0207 234 5800
www.yha.org.uk

The Woodland Trust
Autumn Park, Dysart Road,
Grantham, Lincolnshire NG31 6LL
Tel. 01476 581135
www.woodlandtrust.org.uk

Youth Hostels Association
Trevelyan House, Dimple Road,
Matlock, Derbyshire, DE4 3YH
Tel. 01629 592600
www.yha.org.uk

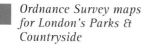

Ordnance Survey maps for London's Parks & Countryside

The area of *London's Parks & Countryside* is covered by Ordnance Survey 1:50 000 (1¼ inches to 1 mile or 2 cm to 1km)

scale Landranger map sheets 166, 167, 176, 177, 178 and 187. These all-purpose maps are packed with information to help you explore the area and show viewpoints, picnic sites, places of interest and caravan and camping sites.

To examine *London's Parks & Countryside* area in more detail and especially if you are planning walks, Ordnance Survey Explorer maps at 1:25 000 (2½ inches to 1 mile or 4cm to 1km) scale are ideal:

146	(Dorking, Box Hill & Reigate)
147	(Sevenoaks & Tonbridge)
161	(London South)
162	(Greenwich & Gravesend)
172	(Chiltern Hills East)
173	(London North)
174	(Epping Forest & Lee Valley)

To get to *London's Parks & Countryside* use the Ordnance Survey OS Travel Map-Route Great Britain at 1:625 000 (1 inch to 10 miles or 4cm to 25 km) scale or Ordnance Survey OS Travel Map-Road 8 (South East England including London).

Ordnance Survey maps and guides are available from most booksellers, stationers and newsagents.

The River Thames at Richmond looking towards Richmond Bridge visited on walk 27

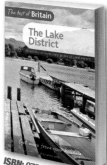
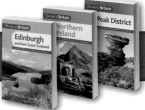